Contemporary
COOKING

Volume 6

Contemporary
COOKING

Volume 6

3M

Contemporary Cooking

Editorial production by James Charlton Associates, Ltd.
New York. Editor-in-Chief, James Charlton; Managing
Editors, Barbara Binswanger, Jennie McGregor; Food
Editors, Inez M. Krech, Betsy Lawrence, Anne Lanigan,
Maria Robbins, Joan Whitman.

Book production and manufacturing consulting by:
Cobb/Dunlop Publishing Services, Inc., New York
Art Direction and interior design by:
Marsha Cohen/Parallelogram

Acknowledgments: Pat Cocklin, Delu PAL International,
Alan Duns, John Elliott, Gus Francisco Photography, Mel-
vin Grey, Gina Harris, Anthony Kay, Paul Kemp, David
Levin, David Meldrum, Roger Phillips, Nick Powell, Iain
Reid, John Turner, Paul Williams, George Wright, Cuisi-
narts, Inc.

Printed and bound in Yugoslavia by CGP Delo.

Library of Congress Cataloging in Publication Data
Main entry under title:

Contemporary Cooking.

    Includes index.
    1. Cookery.   I. Minnesota Mining and Manufacturing
Company.
TX715.C7586   1984   641.5   84-2563
0-88159-500-4   —   (set)
ISBN: 0-88159–005–3

CONTENTS
for the Contemporary Cooking Series

VOLUME 6

Part One

EGG COOKERY II

"Simply to wake just in time to smell coffee and bacon and eggs. . . .
how rarely it happens! But when it does happen—then what a moment, what a morning, what a delight!"
    J. B. Priestley
    Delight

Fried eggs—served up with bacon, sausages or ham; a side dish of home fries, grits; some toast, perhaps a muffin—have been for many years and still remain among the most popular breakfast foods in America. One could venture a guess that more eggs are fried each morning of the year in every coffee shop and luncheonette, in every roadside diner and greasy spoon, than are prepared in any other way. To fry an egg, one might conclude, must be simplicity itself. Almost every summer we get to watch a sweaty news reporter fry an egg right on the sidewalk to show us just how hot it is.

When it comes to the actual process of frying eggs, there seems to be a host of strongly held opinions, not just about the way they should be cooked, but how they should look and taste and even how they should be eaten. A thirteenth-century point of table etiquette (which, incidentally, shows that fried eggs were eaten long before the introduction of the fork) instructs, "Dig not at the fried egg with thumb turned down but move it about with the point of your knife."

Some people like their eggs cooked "over easy" so that the yolk is tucked away under a slightly crisp skin; others insist their eggs be cooked "sunny side up," the yolk a perfect golden globe centered on the sphere of white; some like the edges crisp and brown; others insist the whites must be as pure as driven snow, tooth tender but opaque as milk. Some say that eggs should be fried only in bacon fat; others insist on butter, or drippings from a ham, or olive oil, or lard . . .

Perhaps it is because fried eggs fall into the category of comfort and security foods, those rich with associations of hearth and home and childhood, that most people are so particular about the way they like their eggs. Many an otherwise rational and even-tempered soul has flown into a rage or dissolved in tears of disappointment when eggs that should have been "sunny side up" were served with hardened broken yolks.

It is much easier to define a perfect omelet or a perfect soft-cooked egg in the shell, than it is to sum up all the qualities that make up everyman's perfect fried egg. Perfect fried eggs are a matter of personal taste, informed by heritage, tradition and, often enough, the memory of how we ate them long ago.

"Few women can fry an egg as my mother could," wrote Della Lutes in her memoir of country family life in the 1870s. "Her technique was perfect, and the result was no leathery mass of frizzled white and broken yolk, but an intact globule of limed yellow set in a circle of delicately congealed albumen. She fried eggs in the fat from bacon or ham, whichever happened to be in use. This fat was made hot—sizzling but never smoking; if it was too hot, it was drawn to the back of the stove until there was no danger of browning the thin edge of the white before the yolk was cooked.

"Each egg was broken separately and gently into the sizzling fat, and never were so many introduced . . . that their edges mingled. Then my mother stood by, spooning the hot fat over them until the yolks presented an opaque appearance and the whites were coagulated but not hardened. They were then, at the exact moment of perfection . . . laid on a warm platter along with the ham, rosily tender and faintly browned, or bacon, done to a curl but never to a crisp. An egg fried in this fashion, its qualities and virtues instantly sealed within it by a hot, sweet coating of honest fat, cannot be too great a tax upon the digestive machinery. Numberless were the fried eggs my father consumed, and he bore up under them until well past his eighty-fifth birthday."

Fried eggs are popular elsewhere around the world, although not necessarily cooked the same way and not necessarily for breakfast. Among the many egg dishes in France are *oeufs sur le plat*, eggs baked and served in individual shirred egg dishes, thereby eliminating the possibility of breaking the yolks while transferring the eggs from pan to plate. These eggs are baked at moderate heat. Sometimes the dishes are covered, which creates a small amount of steam that lightly cooks the surface of the eggs and gives them a shiny, mirrored appearance. *Oeufs en cocotte* are also baked in individual dishes, although they have a more delicate texture than shirred eggs. They are set in a pan of water, covered, and baked at low heat.

In France, *oeufs frits* (fried eggs) are deep-fried eggs. Each egg is broken into a cup and gently slid into a deep pan of very hot fat or oil. The egg is rolled over in the fat as it cooks so that the white folds around the yolk and the whole egg puffs up all crisp and golden brown. These eggs are delicious served on a bed of spinach or with a spicy, rich tomato sauce.

Fried eggs are much beloved in Spain, where they are shallow-fried in sizzling olive oil until the whites turn golden brown and very crisp. Although the trimmings sound familiar—spicy *chorizo* sausage, fried potatoes, bread—these eggs are served with wine for lunch or dinner, never for breakfast.

"Nothing," remarked Mark Twain, "helps scenery like ham and eggs," and it is not unlikely that he had in mind fried eggs just like those immortalized by M. F. K. Fisher in *An Alphabet for Gourmets,* under the letter H for Happy:

"When I was a child my Aunt Gwen . . . used to walk my little sister Anne and me up into the hills at sundown. She insisted on pockets. We had to have at least two apiece when we were with her. In one of them, on these twilight promenades, would be some cookies. In the other, oh, deep sensuous delight! would be a fried egg sandwich!" Mrs. Fisher then thoughtfully provides a recipe for Aunt Gwen's Fried Egg Sandwiches, which is divided into four sections. Ingredients (Physical): eggs, drippings, bread, wax paper; Ingredients (Spiritual): equal parts of "hunger and happiness"; Method: wherein the procedure for making the sandwiches is detailed with the warning, "These sandwiches, if properly made and wrapped, are guaranteed, if properly carried in sweater or pinafore pockets, to make large oily stains around them;" and finally the Prescription: they are "To be eaten on top of a hill at sunset, between trios of 'A Wandering Minstrel I' and 'Onward Christian Soldiers,' preferably before adolescence and its priggish queasiness set in."

FRIED, SHIRRED AND BAKED EGGS

There are more ways to use eggs than any other single food. They are cheap, nutritious and very quick to cook, making them the best value for money in the kitchen. Although eggs, including fried eggs, are frequently associated with breakfast, they can form the basis for dishes ranging from elegant first courses to robust suppers.

It is important to remember two things when cooking eggs: Avoid high heat lest you toughen the egg protein, and remember that eggs go on cooking even after they have been removed from heat.

Heat makes an egg solidify, but the white hardens at a lower temperature than the yolk. With accurate timing and cooking at the right temperature, you can produce a perfectly cooked egg with a set white and a still runny yolk, which will break as you start to eat it. Fierce heat will make the egg white spatter; prolonged heat will shrivel the white and harden the yolk to an indigestible state. Diners must wait for eggs, not the eggs for diners. Fortunately, eggs are so quick to cook that you can usually prepare them while the diners are already at the table, making it possible for you to serve the eggs as soon as they are done.

Cracking and Separating Eggs

Not everyone can crack raw eggs with the panache of a conjurer, one in each hand, and get them into a bowl without the yolks breaking or the shells crumbling in on top of the eggs. You do not need to try anything so fancy, as there is a simpler method. It is sensible, in any case, to break each egg separately into a saucer or cup first, then tip it into the mixing bowl or the skillet. In this way there is no waste if one egg out of the batch should be stale, or if the recipe requires whole yolks and one of them breaks, or if the recipe requires egg whites without a speck of yolk. To be sure you have retrieved all the egg, move your thumb inside the half-shell to remove all of the egg white.

To separate eggs by the quickest method, crack the shell, drop the

Fried Eggs, "Sunny Side Up"

1 Place 2 teaspoons butter in a frying pan and heat until moderately hot but not sputtering.

2 Tilt the pan to collect the butter on one side. Slide each egg carefully into the pool of butter.

3 When the egg white begins to cook, set the pan level. With a spatula scrape egg white around the yolk.

4 Spoon a little of the hot butter over the top to cook the upper side of the egg. Cook for 2 to 3 minutes.

5 Lift out each egg, being careful not to break the yolk. Blot on paper towels.

6 Sprinkle salt and pepper on the egg whites only. Serve immediately.

whole egg into your hand and let the egg white run out between your fingers into a bowl. Drop the egg yolk into another bowl. It is easiest to separate eggs when they are cold. For a recipe that requires beaten eggs—whole, yolks or whites—you will gain the most volume if you let the eggs come to room temperature after cracking them open or separating them.

Fried Eggs

There are two methods of frying eggs. They can be shallow-fried to produce a yellow yolk in the center of the white, known to Americans as "sunny side up." Or, after the egg has cooked enough to solidify the bottom, a minute or so, it can be turned over with a spatula to make an egg "over easy," an egg which is cooked on both sides. The yolk is masked with egg white and is more cooked than in the first method.

You can also fry eggs in deep fat as the French do, which gives a puffy golden egg, not flat but rather oval, with the yolk hidden inside the coating of fried egg white.

Shallow-Fried Eggs. For shallow-frying eggs you will need a frying pan large enough to hold as many eggs as needed. A 5-inch pan will be perfect for a single egg; a pan 8 inches across the base will be adequate for 4 eggs. The pan should be of iron or aluminum, with a heavy base. Light metal pans are not satisfactory because they heat unevenly. You will also need a saucer or cup, into which you break the eggs, one at a time, and paper towels for blotting the finished eggs well so they do not take the cooking fat with them to the table. You will also need a spatula.

For shallow-frying the traditional breakfast egg, fresh bacon drippings add a delicious flavor. If you are serving bacon as well, this fat will be conveniently at hand. Lard, vegetable shortening, butter or oils can also be used, but of these only butter adds a good flavor to the eggs. Be careful when frying with butter; it burns at high heat, but eggs should be cooked over low heat in any case.

Deep-Fried Eggs

1 Measure oil into a heavy saucepan large enough to fry 1 egg. Heat oil to 370°F.

2 Break 1 egg into a cup. Holding cup close to saucepan, slide the egg gently into the hot oil.

3 Dip a perforated spoon into the hot oil and gently roll egg over once or twice to enfold the yolk.

4 Fry for 50 to 55 seconds only. Lift out the egg with the perforated spoon and blot on paper towels.

If using fat, put the fat in the pan and heat it. To check whether it is at the right heat for shallow-frying, test-fry a bread cube. It should sizzle for 2 minutes before browning. Adjust the heat until you get it right, then add the eggs. As the white begins to cook, push it around the yolk to make the finished egg a neat round or oval.

When the eggs are done to your taste, lift them with a spatula to the paper towels to drain, then serve without delay. These eggs should not be kept over heat after they are ready, because they will become rubbery. If the eggs are to be served with bacon or other fried accompaniments, cook those first and keep them warm in a low oven until the eggs are ready.

Deep-Fried Eggs. For deep-frying eggs, you will need a small heavy saucepan about 5 inches across the base. You could use a larger deep-

fryer, but that would be wasteful of oil since only 1 egg should be fried at a time. You will also need a saucer and paper towels. The fat to use is a light-textured oil, such as corn or peanut oil. Lard or drippings do not give successful results in deep-frying. Oils reach a much higher temperature before smoking and will not splatter.

Pour the oil into the saucepan and heat it to 370°F on a frying thermometer. If you do not have a thermometer, fry a bread cube. If it browns within 40 seconds after being dropped into the hot oil, the temperature is right. Slide the egg into the fat; use a perforated spoon to turn the egg over as it cooks so the yolk is entirely surrounded by the white. The egg should be done in less than 1 minute. Lift out and blot on paper towels. A deep-fried egg looks attractive, but the white is often rather tough.

Shirred Eggs

Shirred eggs are cooked in shallow baking dishes. These special little dishes can be found in kitchen supply stores; they are round or oval, and may be made of copper, heavy enamel, earthenware, or porcelain-lined cast iron, but the most common are pottery. They are always ovenproof, with a little handle or ear on each side. They are about 1 inch deep, and can be found in two sizes; the small size holds a single egg, the larger holds 2 eggs.

Shirred eggs are baked, but they can be finished in the broiler. This method is one of the simplest ways to prepare eggs, since they are served in the cooking dish. The French name for these eggs is *oeufs sur le plat,* literally, eggs on the dish. Butter is the only fat to use for shirring, since it is served with the finished egg. For 1 egg, melt 1 teaspoon butter in the shirred egg dish, or spread it around the dish. Break the egg into the dish, or slide it into the dish from a saucer, and set the dish on a baking sheet. Bake in a preheated 350°F oven for 10 to 12 minutes, until the egg white is set and the top of the egg shiny. When you have done this a few times, you can determine the exact number of minutes that produces an egg suitable to your taste. Because of the shiny top on these eggs, they are sometimes called *oeufs au miroir,* looking-glass eggs.

Another method is to bake them in a very hot oven, 500°F, for less than 3 minutes. After the first minute, baste the top with an additional teaspoon of melted butter.

When shirred eggs are almost done, they can be finished in the broiler; be sure to sprinkle them with butter, grated cheese, or a suitable sauce such as Mornay. It takes only a minute in the broiler; the high heat can overcook the eggs if continued too long.

Although a shirred egg dish is shallow, it is possible to add other ingredients, such as thin slices of ham or cheese, bacon, anchovy fillets, thin layers of blanched spinach or minced broccoli or sliced scallions. At serving time the finished eggs can be garnished with a tiny ribbon of sauce, parsley or watercress sprigs, scallion rings, and many other garnishes.

Another way to bake the eggs is to cover the dish with foil. This creates a small amount of steam, which cooks a veil of egg white over the yolk, giving it a softer appearance. The exact timing of these eggs depends somewhat on the material of the dish; heavier materials will retain more heat and thus continue to cook the eggs after they are removed from the oven. Be sure to allow for this when timing.

Shirred Eggs

1 Melt 2 teaspoons butter in a shirred egg dish for 2 eggs. Season butter with salt and pepper.

2 Break eggs, one at a time, into a saucer and slide into the buttered dish.

3 Set dish on baking sheet and bake in preheated 350°F oven for 10 to 12 minutes. Cover if desired.

4 After baking, the top should be shiny. Spoon a little sauce around the yolk and garnish with parsley.

Baked Eggs

Baking is a misnomer for this type of cooking, which is closer to poaching and is different from making shirred eggs. Although the eggs are cooked and served in baking dishes, the dishes for baked eggs are deeper than those used for shirred eggs and they are always set in a pan of water. These dishes are called cocottes, a name that can be used for a baking dish of any size, but those for baking eggs are small round or oval pottery dishes, large enough to hold a single egg or 2 eggs. The single-egg size, which holds ½ to ¾ cup and is 1½ to 2 inches deep, is the more common cocotte. The French name for these is *oeufs en cocotte.*

You will need 1 heatproof dish for each egg—ramekins, individual soufflé dishes, or cocottes—and a baking pan, such as a roaster, large enough to hold all the cocottes and deep enough to allow water to reach halfway up the sides of the cocottes. This is an improvisation of a *bain-marie* or water bath, used for cooking and reheating egg dishes and delicate egg-based sauces

Eggs in Cocottes with Cream

1 Butter cocottes and place in a large baking pan. Add boiling water to come halfway up sides of cocottes.

2 Slide 1 egg into each cocotte, being careful not to break the yolk. Season the whites only.

3 Place baking pan over low heat and let the water simmer gently for 2 minutes.

4 Pour 1 tablespoon heavy cream over the white of egg in each little cocotte.

5 Cover pan with a sheet of foil and place in a preheated 325°F oven for 10 to 12 minutes.

6 Lift dishes out of the water bath. Wipe the dishes quickly, and serve without delay.

that would curdle over direct heat. You will also need a sheet of foil to cover the pan.

The layer of egg white in a cocotte is thicker than that in a shirred-egg dish; consequently it needs slower cooking at lower heat, which is provided by the insulating water surrounding the cocotte and the lower oven heat. These eggs have a more delicate texture than shirred eggs.

Like shirred eggs, eggs in cocottes cannot be kept waiting but should be served as soon as done, for the eggs will continue to cook in the retained heat of the dishes.

For the simplest procedure, butter the cocotte, break an egg into it, and season. To add moisture, pour 1 tablespoon cream over the egg, or additional butter. Set the cocottes in a large pan and pour in enough boiling water to reach halfway, about 1 inch, up the sides of the cocottes. The pan can be set over heat on top of the stove to bring the water back to a boil, or it can be put directly into the preheated 325°F oven. Cover the pan holding the cocottes with a sheet of foil and bake for 10 to 12 minutes. Be careful when removing the foil cover not to let any water fall into the eggs.

The possible variations on this simple procedure are many. The cocottes can be lined with minced chicken, chicken hash, a vegetable purée, a thick sauce, or even mashed potatoes or rice. The egg in the cocotte can be garnished with vegetables, mushrooms, cheese, chicken livers; it can be covered with a sauce, or it can be sprinkled with cheese and browned under the broiler.

A Hint for Cooking Utensils Used with Eggs

Eggs stain silver and silver-plated cutlery. Clean cutlery immediately after staining. Use homemade paste made of salt and a little water, or use a good silver polish such as Tarni-Shield® Silver Cleaner. If you use the salt paste, apply it to the stains and leave for 15 to 20 minutes. Wash off either polish and buff the cutlery with a cloth.

Shirred Eggs with Prosciutto and Cheese

4 portions

2 teaspoons butter
4 thin slices of prosciutto or
   other ham

4 ounces mozzarella cheese
4 large eggs
   salt and pepper

Preheat oven to 350°F. Using 1 teaspoon butter, lightly coat a shallow ovenproof dish that will hold 4 raw eggs in one layer. Lay the slices of ham in the dish in an even layer. Fold them if they are large but do not overlap them. Cut the cheese into thin slices and cover the ham with the cheese. Break 1 egg carefully over each cheese and ham stack, keeping the yolks well separated. Season the eggs lightly with salt and pepper. Top each egg with a bit of the remaining butter. Bake for 12 minutes, until eggs are just set. Serve very hot, from the dish.

Eggs Baked with Chicken and Tomatoes

6 portions

1 tablespoon butter
1 large tomato
4 ounces cooked boneless
   white meat of chicken

6 eggs
½ teaspoon salt
¼ teaspoon black pepper
1 teaspoon paprika

Preheat oven to 350°F. Butter 6 cocotte dishes. Wash and core the tomato and cut 6 thick slices from it. Mince the chicken. Put a slice of tomato in each buttered cocotte and put an equal portion of the minced chicken on top. Break 1 egg into each dish and sprinkle with salt and pepper. Cover the dishes with buttered wax paper. Place the cocottes in a roasting pan with enough hot water to come halfway up the sides of the dishes. Slide into the preheated oven and bake for 10 minutes.

Remove dishes from the oven. Sprinkle paprika over the eggs and serve at once, in the dishes.

Eggs in Brioches

4 portions

4 brioches or soft rolls	salt and pepper
4 large eggs	butter

Preheat oven to 375°F. Remove the tops of the brioches or rolls and set aside. Use a spoon to remove about 2 tablespoons dough from the center of each roll to make a hole for 1 egg. Be careful not to break the sides of the rolls. Place rolls on a baking sheet and carefully drop an egg into each one. Season eggs with salt and pepper. Top each egg with a small piece of butter. Replace the tops of the brioches or rolls. Bake in the oven for about 8 minutes, until egg whites have set.

Baked Eggs in Rice

4 portions

1½ cups cooked rice	½ cup grated cheese
2 tablespoons butter, melted	4 large eggs
½ cup light cream or half-and-half	¼ cup bread crumbs
few grains of cayenne pepper	4 teaspoons butter

Preheat oven to 375°F. Combine the rice with the melted butter and ¼ cup of the cream. If the rice is cold, heat it over low heat. Add the cayenne. Line the bottom and sides of 4 cocottes with the rice. Sprinkle half of the grated cheese over the rice. Gently break 1 egg into each dish. Cover each egg with 1 tablespoon cream, then with 1 tablespoon bread crumbs. Dot 1 teaspoon of raw butter on each egg and sprinkle eggs with remaining cheese.

Place the cocottes in a shallow pan and add enough boiling water to come halfway up the sides of the dishes. Bake for about 12 minutes, until the eggs are set.

Baked Eggs with Broccoli

4 portions

3 tablespoons butter	5 tablespoons cream
1 tablespoon grated onion	4 extra-large eggs
2 cups chopped cooked broccoli	salt and pepper
pinch of grated nutmeg	4 tablespoons grated Gruyère or other mild cheese

Preheat oven to 325°F. Melt 2 tablespoons of the butter in a saucepan over moderate heat. Sauté the onion in the butter for 2 minutes. Add the chopped broccoli, the nutmeg and 1 tablespoon of the cream. Cook for 2 minutes. Butter 4 cocottes with remaining butter and line the bottom and sides of each cocotte with one quarter of the broccoli mixture.

Break 1 egg into each of the broccoli-lined dishes; sprinkle lightly with salt and pepper. Spoon 1 tablespoon of cream over each egg and sprinkle with 1 tablespoon grated cheese. Place the cocottes in a roasting pan and pour enough boiling water into the pan to come halfway up the sides. Bake for about 12 minutes, until the eggs are set.

Eggs Bel Paese

4 portions

8 ounces lean bacon	¼ teaspoon salt
2 slices of white bread	⅛ teaspoon black pepper
1 tablespoon butter	4 thin slices of bel paese cheese
8 large eggs	

Preheat oven to 375°F. Dice the bacon. Cut crusts from bread slices and cut bread into small cubes. Melt the butter in a small frying pan over moderate heat. Add the diced bacon and bread cubes. Fry them, stirring, for 6 to 8 minutes, until they are crisp and lightly browned. Remove pan from heat.

Place equal amounts of bacon and bread cubes in 4 individual baking dishes, or large shirred egg dishes. Break 2 eggs into each dish. Sprinkle salt and pepper over the eggs. Place a slice of cheese on top of each dish of eggs. The cheese will not completely cover the eggs, but after baking for 15 minutes it will spread. Place the dishes in the center of the oven and bake for 10 to 15 minutes, until the eggs are just set and the cheese has melted and spread. Remove dishes from the oven and serve immediately.

Baked Eggs with Frankfurters

4 to 6 portions

1	medium-size onion	8	frankfurters
2	medium-size potatoes	¼	cup olive oil
2	ounces cooked ham	¼	teaspoon dried basil
1	small green pepper	6	large eggs
1	cup canned peeled	1	teaspoon salt
	tomatoes	½	teaspoon black pepper

Peel and chop onion and potatoes. Dice the ham. Wash and halve the pepper, discard stem, seeds and ribs, and chop the pepper. Drain and chop the tomatoes. Cut frankfurters into ½-inch slices.

Preheat oven to 450°F. Heat the oil in a large frying pan over moderate heat. Add onion and potatoes and cook, stirring occasionally, for 5 minutes. Add the ham, green pepper, tomatoes, frankfurters and basil. Cook, stirring occa-sionally, for 15 minutes. Remove pan from heat and spoon the mixture into a 6-cup baking dish. Smooth the top of the mixture with a spatula.

Break the eggs on top of the mixture and sprinkle them with the salt and pepper. Place the dish in the upper part of the oven and bake for 8 to 10 minutes, until the whites of the eggs are set. Serve at once, from the baking dish.

Irish Fried Eggs

4 portions

2 large tomatoes
2 tablespoons butter
4 slices of bacon

4 large eggs
2 cups mashed potatoes, hot

Preheat broiler to medium. Wash and core tomatoes, and cut them into halves. Melt the butter in a heavy skillet and gently sauté the tomatoes on both sides. Remove tomatoes from the skillet and set aside. In another pan, fry the bacon until crisp.

Meanwhile, fry the eggs in the pan used for the toma-toes. Transfer eggs to a flameproof platter, placing them in a line down the center. Put the tomato slices along one side and the bacon on the other. Fill a pastry bag with the mashed potatoes and pipe them around the edge of the platter. Slide the platter under the broiler for about 2 minutes, until the top of the potatoes is golden brown.

Baked Eggs Espagnole

4 portions

1 large onion
1 garlic clove
1¾ cups canned peeled
tomatoes
2 chorizo sausages
1 small green pepper
3 tablespoons olive oil

2 tablespoons chopped
pimiento
1 teaspoon salt
1 teaspoon black pepper
½ teaspoon dried orégano
8 eggs

Peel onion, cut into thin slices, and separate slices into rings. Peel and mince the garlic. Chop the tomatoes, reserving the can juice. Cut sausages into thick slices; remove casing if you wish. Wash and halve the pepper, discard stem, seeds and ribs, and cut pepper into thin slices.

Preheat oven to 400°F. Heat the oil in a large frying pan over moderate heat. When oil is hot, add onion rings and garlic and sauté, stirring occasionally, for 5 to 7 minutes, until onion rings are soft and translucent but not browned. Add the tomatoes with the can juices, the sausage slices, green pepper, 1 tablespoon of the pimiento, the salt, pepper and orégano. Reduce heat to moderately low and cook for 10 minutes, stirring occasionally. Remove pan from heat and turn the mixture into a shallow ovenproof dish.

Break the eggs on top of the mixture and garnish with remaining pimiento. Place the dish in the oven and bake for about 15 minutes, until the egg whites are set and the yolks still runny. Remove the dish from the oven and serve at once.

Baked Eggs Flamenco

4 portions

1	medium-size onion	¼	teaspoon black pepper
2	garlic cloves	⅛	teaspoon cayenne pepper
8	ounces lean bacon	1	tablespoon chopped fresh parsley
2	small red peppers	1	cup canned whole corn kernels
6	medium-size tomatoes		
4	ounces mushrooms	4	large eggs
¼	cup olive oil		
½	teaspoon salt		

Peel onion and cut into thin slices. Peel garlic and put through a press into the onion. Dice the bacon. Wash and halve peppers, discard stems, seeds and ribs, and chop peppers. Blanch and peel the tomatoes and cut into thin slices. Wipe mushrooms with a damp cloth, trim base of stems, and slice caps and stems.

Preheat oven to 350°F. Heat the oil in a large frying pan over moderate heat. Add onion and garlic and sauté, stirring occasionally, for 5 to 7 minutes, until onion is soft but not browned. Add diced bacon and chopped red peppers to the pan and cook, stirring, for 10 to 12 minutes, until peppers are soft. Stir in the tomatoes, mushrooms, salt, black pepper, cayenne and parsley. Continue cooking for 5 minutes, until tomatoes are reduced to a pulp. Stir in the corn kernels and remove pan from the heat.

Pour the mixture into a 6-cup baking dish. Using the back of a spoon, make 4 small depressions in the vegetable mixture. Break 1 egg into each depression. Place the dish in the center of the oven and bake for 15 minutes, or until the eggs have set. Serve hot, from the baking dish.

Ranchers' Eggs

6 portions

2	garlic cloves	¼	teaspoon black pepper
2	medium-size onions	¼	teaspoon ground coriander
6	tomatoes	12	large eggs
2	ounces canned pimientos	6	ounces Cheddar cheese,
1	green chili pepper		grated (1½ cups)
1	tablespoon olive oil	1	tablespoon butter
1	teaspoon sugar	¼	teaspoon chili powder
½	teaspoon salt		

Peel and crush garlic cloves. Peel and chop onions. Blanch and peel tomatoes, chop them, and remove as many seeds as possible. Drain and chop the pimientos. Wearing rubber or plastic gloves, halve the chili pepper, discard stem, seeds and ribs, and mince the pepper.

Preheat oven to 450°F. Heat the oil in a large frying pan over moderate heat. Add garlic and onions and sauté, stirring occasionally, until onions are soft and translucent but not browned. Add the tomatoes, pimientos, chili pepper, sugar, salt, black pepper and coriander to the pan. Reduce heat to low and simmer the mixture, stirring frequently, for 15 to 20 minutes, until it is soft and pulpy. Remove pan from heat and transfer the mixture to a large baking dish.

With the back of a tablespoon make 12 hollows in the mixture. Break 1 egg into each hollow. Sprinkle the cheese over the eggs. Dot the butter over the cheese and sprinkle with the chili powder. Place the baking dish in the center of the oven and bake the eggs for 6 to 8 minutes, until the cheese is golden brown and the eggs have set. Remove dish from oven and serve eggs immediately, from the baking dish.

Eggs with Bacon and Mushrooms

4 portions

8	ounces mushrooms		salt and pepper
1	tablespoon butter	4	large eggs
4	slices of bacon		

Wipe the mushrooms with a damp cloth, trim base of stems, and chop caps and stems. Melt the butter in a frying pan over low heat. Add bacon and fry gently on one side. Add the chopped mushrooms and continue frying gently for 2 minutes longer. Drain off excess fat. Season mushrooms generously with salt and pepper. Turn the bacon over. Break the eggs, one at a time, into a saucer and slide them into the pan. Cover the pan and cook over gentle heat for 4 minutes, until egg whites are set.

Eggs Baked in Tomatoes

4 portions

4	large ripe tomatoes	2	tablespoons butter
	salt and pepper	4	tablespoons grated cheese
4	large eggs		

Preheat oven to 350°F. Wash the tomatoes and slice off the tops. Scoop out the pulp (use for another recipe). Invert the tomatoes on paper towels to drain for 10 minutes. Turn up and sprinkle the insides with a little salt and pepper. Place the tomatoes in a buttered shallow flameproof dish.

Break 1 egg into each hollowed-out tomato, sprinkle the egg with a little salt and pepper, and dot with butter. Bake for about 15 minutes. Preheat broiler to medium.

Remove baking dish from the oven, sprinkle cheese on the tops of the tomatoes and eggs, and slide under the broiler until the cheese is brown.

Baked Eggs Veronese

6 portions

3	tablespoons butter, melted	½	teaspoon black pepper
¾	cup bread crumbs	½	cup grated Parmesan or
1	pound mozzarella cheese		Romano cheese
6	large eggs		

Preheat oven to 400°F. Combine melted butter and bread crumbs and spread them evenly over the bottom of a shallow baking dish large enough for 6 eggs. Cut the mozzarella cheese into thin slices.

Spread half of the cheese slices over the crumb layer in the baking dish; overlap the cheese slices if necessary. Break the eggs, one at a time, into a saucer or bowl and gently slide them onto the cheese slices, spacing them evenly. Cover with remaining slices of cheese, then sprinkle with black pepper and grated cheese. Bake in the preheated oven for 15 minutes, until the egg whites are set.

Baked Farmer's Eggs

4 portions

4	medium-size potatoes	½	cup grated Gruyère or
5	tablespoons butter		other mild cheese
1	teaspoon salt	8	large eggs
½	teaspoon pepper	½	cup cream

Preheat oven to 375°F. Peel potatoes and cut lengthwise into thin slices. Melt the butter in a heavy skillet over moderate heat and sauté the potatoes, turning them often, until they are browned. Sprinkle potatoes with salt and pepper and transfer them to a shallow baking dish. Cover potato slices with grated cheese.

Break the eggs gently and place them on top of the cheese. Sprinkle with a little more salt and pepper and spoon 1 tablespoon cream over each egg. Bake for about 10 minutes, until the eggs are set.

16

Eggs in Potato Nests

6 portions

3 large potatoes, baked
4 ounces butter
1 cup milk or light cream, hot

salt and pepper
6 large eggs
6 tablespoons grated cheese

Preheat oven to 350°F. Split the baked potatoes lengthwise and scoop out the pulp, leaving enough potato to keep a firm shell. Reserve the potato shells. Put potato pulp in a mixing bowl and beat in 6 tablespoons of the butter. Beat in the hot milk or cream until the potatoes are light and fluffy. Season them with salt and pepper. Fill the shells with the mashed potato mixture, building up the sides and leaving the center

hollow to make a nest. Gently break 1 egg into each potato half, season with salt and pepper, and dot with 1 teaspoon butter. Bake for about 12 minutes, until eggs are set. Preheat broiler to medium.

Sprinkle the eggs and tops of potatoes with the grated cheese, and brown under the broiler.

Oeufs en Cocotte Pascal

4 portions

2 teaspoons butter
fresh parsley, chives, tarragon and chervil
¼ cup heavy cream

2 teaspoons prepared Dijon-style mustard
½ teaspoon salt
¼ teaspoon black pepper
4 large eggs

Preheat oven to 325°F. Butter 4 cocotte dishes. Mince enough of the herbs to make 2 tablespoons. Pour the cream into a small saucepan. Add the mustard, salt, pepper and herbs. Warm the sauce over low heat, stirring until it is smooth.

Break the eggs, one at a time, into a saucer and slide each egg into a buttered cocotte. Put the cocottes in a baking

pan and add enough boiling water to come halfway up the sides of the dishes. Cook over low heat on top of the stove for 2 minutes so the water simmers gently. Divide the cream and herb mixture among the eggs and cover the pan with foil. Transfer pan to the oven and bake for 10 minutes. Serve the eggs in the cocottes.

Portuguese Eggs in Cocottes

4 portions

1	medium-size onion			black pepper
4	tablespoons butter			pinch of dried orégano
3	medium-size tomatoes			salt
1	teaspoon sugar		4	large eggs
1	tablespoon wine vinegar		2½	tablespoons light cream or
½	teaspoon Tabasco®			half-and-half

Preheat oven to 325°F. Peel and mince the onion. Melt 2 tablespoons of the butter in a skillet and sauté the onion until translucent but not browned. Blanch and peel the tomatoes, chop them, and remove as many seeds as possible. Add 1 tablespoon water to the skillet and put in the tomatoes, sugar, vinegar and Tabasco. Bring to a boil, stirring with a wooden spoon. Simmer until tomatoes are soft, about 5 minutes, adding more water if necessary. Season with a little black pepper. Stir the orégano and salt to taste into the tomato mixture.

Butter 4 cocotte dishes with remaining butter and put the cocottes in a roasting pan. Distribute the hot tomato mixture evenly among the 4 cocottes, covering the base. Slide 1 egg into each dish, taking care not to break the yolks, so the egg sits on top of the tomato mixture. Spoon a scant 2 teaspoons cream over the white of each egg. Salt lightly on the whites only. Carefully pour boiling water into the roasting pan to reach halfway up the sides of the cocottes. Cover the roasting pan with foil and transfer it to the oven. Bake for 8 to 10 minutes, until the whites are set but the yolks are still runny.

Lift the dishes out of the water. Wipe each one carefully. Serve with French bread.

Part Two

ROASTING MEATS

For the Stone Age man, without means of preserving meat, the roast—that is to say, a slaughtered animal or any significant joint thereof—cooked, however crudely, over an open fire, represented a miraculous triumph over the almost constant reality of near starvation. If it was a tribute to the manly skills of hunting, and to the gods who meted out such successes, it was also an apt reflection of man's social nature. Animals of large size were considerably easier prey for men hunting cooperatively, and the resulting abundant but perishable food supply could only have been consumed efficiently by a group that had achieved at the least a rudimentary talent for sharing.

As human society progressed from hunting and gathering to farming and herding domesticated animals, the killing and roasting of those animals remained an essentially male activity that was reserved for occasions when clans were gathered, whether for the purposes of religious ceremony, like the paschal lamb, or personal celebration, like the famous fatted calf, or for simple hospitality.

Hospitality (which is, in fact, rarely simple) has always been understood as a more or less conscious display of wealth and status as well as a pious obligation or a sincere expression of generosity. Thus feasts, whether religious in nature as the word originally implied or purely secular as they now often are, generally involved a sacrifice of what was most dear. In ancient Greece, for instance, game of various sorts was fairly plentiful, but only a person of princely station could afford to keep cattle, which were in effect a kind of currency. The host of a truly great feast would be expected literally and personally to sacrifice a part of his wealth; that is, he would himself slaughter an ox, which would then be roasted and consumed after an appropriate portion was offered up in smoke to the gods. If it was suspected that the gods required more appeasement than usual, the roasting flames would be allowed to consume the entire ox, thus effecting a holocaust or "whole burning."

Pressing circumstances or special need of divine favor might even, for the very rich, call for a hecatomb, the sacrifice of 100 cattle at once.

The Olympian gods may have been a good deal hungrier in the Middle Ages, for though food was no doubt wasted, very little was offered up in the form of burnt sacrifices. Nevertheless, the roasted joint, not to mention the whole suckling pig, lamb, goat, hind, or even cow, was very much in evidence, if not on the peasants' tables then as part of the largess that every lord showed his vassals. One can hardly conjure up a scene of baronial splendor without imagining huge roasted joints of venison or some such, gone at with boisterous gusto by a raucous crowd of forkless men-at-arms.

The fact is, there has hardly been a century in recorded history when diners have not gathered, raucously or otherwise, around a roasted joint of meat. There is evidence that the Egyptians were keeping domesticated cattle for roasting nearly 5,500 years ago. Goats and sheep have been domesticated for nearly as long, and pigs—well, collectively, pigs have spent more time turning over a bed of hot coals than have all the other domesticated animals combined, and that in spite of the fact the Muslim and Hebrew religions shun the eating of their flesh. A much despised animal is the pig, but much praised, too, and never more lovingly than by Charles Lamb in his famous *Dissertation on Roast Pig:*

> *He must be roasted.* . . . There is no flavor comparable, I will contend to that of the crisp, tawny, well-watched, not over-roasted, *crackling,* as it is well called—the very teeth are invited to their share of the pleasure at this banquet in overcoming the coy, brittle resistance—with the adhesive oleaginous—O call it not fat! but an indefinable sweetness growing up to it—the tender blossoming of fat—fat cropped in the bud—taken in the shoot—in the first innocence—the cream and quintessence of the child-pig's yet pure food—the lean, no lean, but a kind of animal manna—or, rather, fat and lean (if it must be so) so blended and running into each other, that both together make but one ambrosian result or common substance.

It has been pointed out that, while the boiling of meat was the most economical use of it (what was not eaten as meat was had as soup the next day) and therefore a mainstay of the harder-pressed classes, the roasting of meat was, with its reckless squandering of fat in the flames, an aristocratic act. All that was, no doubt, true at a time when roasting (the cooking of food by exposure to intense, dry heat) essentially meant broiling on a spit over live coals. Modern roasting, of course, is largely done in an oven with the meat trussed and resting on a roasting rack, with a pan to catch the drippings. (A pot roast is really no roast at all, but rather a form of braised meat.)

In modern times, particularly in this country, we are lucky to have meat available widely and at prices that most people can afford. Still, there remains something special and festive about roasting a large piece of meat. Its very size reminds us of the bounty to which even the least of us may aspire occasionally, and calms the fear of need that even the greatest of us suffer. Of its own accord it prompts generosity and puts us in mind of hospitality and sharing. What jaded palate would not consider with just a touch of awe and joy the serving up of a crown roast of lamb, or a whole suckling pig, a standing rib roast or a saddle of veal?

ROASTING MEATS

True roasting, either oven-roasting or the earlier spit-roasting, is a dry-heat method in which all sides of the meat are cooked by hot air. As a result it is not suitable for lean meats, cuts with a lot of connective tissue, or any cut that lacks natural internal fats.

Choosing Meat

Most Americans buy their meat at the supermarket, where the enormous array of cuts can be confusing. If you are lucky enough to have a good butcher, ask questions; you will learn something about the intricacies of butchering. For those not so fortunate, acquiring a basic understanding of the U.S. meat grading system and the most-used cuts available will enable you to choose well from any meat case. The voluntary meat identity labeling system, which is being used more and more, identifies the wholesale cut as well as the retail cut, and eventually the same retail name should be used all through the country.

The U.S. Department of Agriculture has established an inspection system that goes a long way to ensure that the meat you buy is wholesome, and of acceptable quality and freshness. The grading system indicates quality of meat—its conformation, tenderness, juiciness, flavor, and the amount of usable meat on the carcass. There are 8 grades for beef, 6 grades for veal, 5 grades for lamb, but only 3 grades of each are used by consumers. Pork is treated differently; its grades are numbers rather than names.

Veal, lamb and pork are slaughtered young, so they are naturally tender, and the grading is less significant than it is for beef. Nevertheless, look for PRIME and CHOICE veal and lamb if you are planning to roast your meat, and for Number 1 or 2 for good pork.

PRIME. The best-quality beef comes from young, specially fed cattle. The meat is well marbled with fat, firm but tender. PRIME meat is not found everywhere; it is sold to butcher shops rather than supermarkets. Much PRIME meat is sold to restaurants.

CHOICE. This is the most commonly available high-quality grade of beef. It is less marbled than PRIME beef, but still very tender. CHOICE grade has 5 subcategories that are rated according to leanness. The leanest are not suitable for open roasting but are fine for covered roasting.

GOOD. Meat graded GOOD is adequate for many cooking methods, but roasting is generally not one of them; meats of GOOD grade have less fat and are thus less tender than CHOICE. However, certain naturally tender cuts, such as rib roasts and filet, are tender enough to roast even in GOOD meats.

Quantities. As a general rule, you will need from 4 to 8 ounces of boneless meat per person, depending on appetite, and 6 to 12 ounces per person of cuts with an average amount of bone. Cuts that weigh less than 3 pounds shrink too much in roasting, but they can be roasted if care is taken to choose a pan just large enough for the meat and to provide moisture or additional fat.

Storing Meats

Fresh Meat. All meat must be refrigerated. When you get the meat home, unwrap it, place it on a plate or in a bowl, and cover with a cloth or plastic wrap. Do not make the covering airtight, but allow a little air to enter and circulate. Some refrigerators have a special meat storage drawer in which you can place unwrapped meat.

As a rough guide, large beef roasts can be stored for about 5 days, smaller cuts for 2 to 3 days. Veal will keep for a day or two, large cuts of pork and lamb for up to 3 days.

Frozen Meat. Uncooked frozen beef and lamb, in large pieces, well wrapped, can be stored safely for 6 months; veal loses flavor after 3 months, and pork can develop rancidity after 4 months. Small pieces, or ground meats, can be stored for 1 month.

Cooked Meat. Cool cooked meat as quickly as possible; if the weather is hot, set the container in a bowl of ice cubes to speed cooling. Wrap the meat, uncarved, as soon as it is cold. Wrapping prevents drying of the meat, which has already been dried in the cooking process. Wrap meat with foil or plastic wrap, but do not make the package airtight. Store in the refrigerator at once and plan to use it within 3 days.

Preparing Meat for Roasting

Fresh meat for roasting should be removed from the refrigerator long enough for it to reach room temperature before cooking; 2 to 3 hours is usually long enough, but the time depends on the size of the piece of meat. However, pork and variety meats should remain in the refrigerator until you are ready to cook them; for these meats the risk of spoilage at higher temperatures is great.

Frozen meat, if it is a large cut, should be thawed before it is roasted as this improves the texture. Large pieces of frozen meat are difficult to roast successfully if they have not been thawed; the outside will probably be overcooked and the inside will remain uncooked. Smaller pieces may be roasted unthawed if necessary.

Some cuts of meat come with their natural outer coating of fat; others are sold rolled and barded with fat. Any very lean meat can be barded or larded.

Barding or Outerlarding. This process is used for lean cuts, removed from the bone and rolled, and for other lean cuts that may be on the bone. It means that a protective layer of fat is wrapped around the meat and tied at intervals with string; the fat keeps the meat moist with a minimum of basting, which is necessary if the meat is to be cooked by high-temperature methods.

The fat used may be unsalted pork fatback. A better choice for beef is beef fat cut from around the flank. Your butcher can cut the fat into thin slices and flatten it between sheets of wax paper. Salt pork and bacon are not desirable because of the high salt content.

Larding. This is a method of inserting fat strips into a lean cut of meat. It improves the flavor, keeps the meat succulent, and promotes even cooking. Larding is recommended when roasting a cut without much internal fat, such as cuts from the beef round, although it is more often done for meat to be braised. The best fat to use is unsalted pork fatback, but salt pork can be used if the added salt is agreeable. Probably the best choice is fat from the same kind of meat, if that is available. You will need about 4 ounces of fat for a 5-pound roast. Thin strips are cut from the fat; these are called lardoons. Lardoons may be rolled in a mixture of seasoning and spices, or they may be marinated in brandy and herbs to give extra flavor.

To cut lardoons, chill the fat for several hours. Warm the knife you use in hot water. Cut slices about ¼-inch wide and then cut the slices into ¼-inch strips. A larding needle has a long hollow in which the strip of fat rests; the needle is inserted into the meat, then carefully withdrawn, leaving the fat in place.

Seasoning and Flavoring. Meats can be seasoned or not, but it is better not to do it. Seasoning on the fatty surfaces will melt as the fat melts and carry seasoning to the bottom of the pan, where it can burn and spoil the flavor of the gravy. Never salt any cut surface, as salt draws out juices and can make the outer portions flavorless and dry. Herbs and garlic can be inserted into slits, but every hole you make allows meat juices to escape. For a mild garlic taste, rub the meat all over with the cut surface of a garlic clove. Herbs can be placed around and under the meat. The fat you use will also affect the taste. All fats can be used, but avoid butter if cooking by a high-temperature method, as butter burns at high heat.

Roasting Methods

Open roasting. There are three possible approaches to open roasting: searing, high-temperature roasting, and low-temperature roasting. High-temperature roasting is suitable only for tender, well-marbled cuts, and low-temperature roasting is in general preferred for all meats.

Put about 3 tablespoons fat in a roasting pan and put the pan in the oven when you start to preheat it. When the correct temperature is reached, remove the pan, put a rack in it, and set the meat on the rack. The rack lifts the meat above the bottom of the pan so that it does not sit in the fat released by the meat; the fat in the pan bottom becomes very hot and without the rack could burn the bottom of the meat. Spoon the hot fat over the meat, then place the pan in the center of the oven. The hot fat helps to make an instant seal on the outside of the meat, keeping in the juices.

Roasting Ribs of Beef

1 Preheat oven to 500°F. Set the beef on the rib bones in the roasting pan.

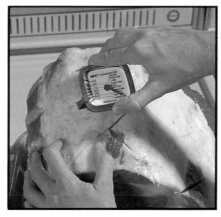

2 Set arrow of meat thermometer at desired temperature and insert into thickest part of beef, not touching bone or fat.

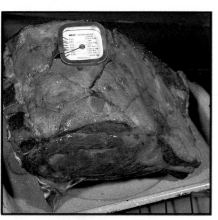

3 Roast beef for 10 minutes, then reduce oven heat to 350°F. When thermometer has almost reached the arrow, turn off oven.

4 Let beef rest in the turned-off oven or other warm place for 15 minutes before carving.

Baste the meat regularly with the fat and juices from the pan. Use a heat-proof spoon or a bulb baster. Roasting tends to dry out the meat, so even larded meat needs some basting. For barded meat, basting may be omitted.

You may choose rare, medium, or well-done meat, but it is usual to serve beef rare and lamb is often preferred that way. The charts give the various roasting times.

Searing Method. This method is suitable only for tender cuts of beef. It seals in the flavor and juices. The meat is started in an oven preheated to 475° to 500°F and roasted for 10 minutes. The temperature is then reduced to 350°F. To reduce the temperature quickly, leave the oven door open when you baste the meat. Cook at 350°F for the rest of the estimated time.

It is possible to cook PRIME and CHOICE beef by searing the roast at 500°F, turning off the oven heat, and then leaving the meat in the oven, without opening the door, to cook for the rest of the time as the oven cools.

The searing method is also good for cooking frozen meats. Start off roasting at 450°F for 25 minutes to seal it; this also helps to evaporate excess moisture. Reduce heat to 350°F

and cook until the internal temperature reaches the correct degree. It is difficult to give a general figure for minutes per pound, as it depends on the cut and the size. Insert the thermometer as soon as the meat has softened enough to make it possible.

Thawed frozen meat can be cooked by whichever method you prefer.

High-Temperature Method. This method is suitable for tender cuts. Less tender cuts can be cooked this way on occasion if they have been aged and marinated. Roasts cooked at high temperature have the best flavor, but the meat does shrink during cooking.

Low-Temperature Method. This method makes meat fibers more tender and causes less shrinkage. Generally, this is the best way to roast all high-grade cuts of meat. Reserve the high-temperature method for an emergency procedure when you are short of time.

Testing for Doneness

Meat Thermometer. A meat thermometer is useful for indicating the internal temperature of the meat.

Stick the pointed end of the thermometer into the thickest part of the meat, not touching bone or fat, before putting the meat in the oven. Just before the desired internal temperature is reached, remove the roast from the oven; it will continue to cook in the retained heat and will reach the correct temperature as it "rests" before carving. Some meats come pre-packaged with temperature gauges, such as the Dun-Rite® Pop-up Timer.

A thermometer can be used for frozen meats only after defrosting and it is an important tool for cooking thawed meat properly. If you are obliged to cook meat from the frozen state, wait to insert the thermometer until it has cooked for about half of the time. Then make a hole for the thermometer with a skewer, and insert the thermometer at once, to avoid losing too much juice.

Meat Skewers. Piercing the meat with a skewer and looking at the color of the juices gives some indication of how well done the meat is, although it is not an accurate method. If the juices are red, the meat is underdone and requires longer cooking. If juices are slightly rosy, the meat is rare; if juices are colorless, the meat is well done. Do not be tempted to do a num-

Carving Roast Ribs of Beef, Method I

1 With the left hand protected with paper toweling, grasp the rib bones to keep the roast steady.

2 Slice down to the backbone, then turn the blade to the right to release meat from bone.

3 Slide the blade between the thin edge of the slice and the rib bone.

Carving Roast Ribs of Beef, Method II

1 Hold the roast steady with the fork between the rib bones.

2 Carve across the top surface evenly, using a sawing motion.

3 Free the slice by running the knife tip along the inner side of the rib bone.

ber of tests; each time the skewer is inserted, juices are lost from the meat.

Fingertip Test. For meats to be eaten rare, the fingertip method is better, though it requires some practice. Press the cooked meat with your fingertips. If the meat feels soft and springy, it is underdone. If the meat feels firm and does not yield, it is well done or perhaps overdone. Experience will teach you to recognize the degree of rareness you prefer.

Carving

Good carving is an economy. A skilled carver makes a roast go further than one who merely hacks at it. If possible, always plan time for the meat to "rest" in a warm place for 10 to 15 minutes before carving. This allows meat juices to be redistributed, so they will not be lost in carving. Also it makes the meat firmer and easier to carve evenly.

The first essential is a sharp long-bladed carving knife. The blade should be sharpened before each use, then wiped with a clean cloth to remove any metal dust. The second essential is a carving fork fitted with a guard; this protects the carver's hand if the knife should slip accidentally.

Place the meat firmly on a large warmed platter. A wooden board can be used; spiked boards are particularly good for holding a roast firmly and preventing slipping. Boards or dishes with channels and hollows to catch meat juices also have advantages.

Use the knife with a gentle sawing movement so that it passes smoothly through the meat. Whenever possible, carve across the grain of the meat, thus shortening the fibers so the meat is more tender to eat.

BEEF

America has often been called the land of beef and plenty, and no wonder, when you consider how popular this meat is. Even in times of changing dietary habits, meat means beef to many people, and anything else is secondary.

Beef that has been hung in a cool room for 5 to 7 days will be more flavorful. If you buy a roast that has not been aged in this way, keep it in your refrigerator for 2 or 3 days before cooking. Even this brief aging will help to tenderize it.

Look for firm red flesh, well marbled with white or ivory fat. Avoid beef that has a layer of gristle between the muscle and outer fat, or with yellow fat; these indicate that the animal is old.

Chuck. Two cuts from this portion can be roasted: the blade roast, the first cut of the shoulder, and the cross-rib roast.

Rib. This section produces rib roasts, standing with bones, and rolled roasts, as well as the succulent rib-eye roast, all suitable for open roasting.

Tenderloin. The tenderloin or filet of beef runs through the short loin and the sirloin. It is the tenderest, thus most expensive, cut. Whole tenderloins or large pieces can be roasted; the butt end is especially suited to high-temperature roasting. Cuts from the tenderloin include the chateaubriand, a double-thick cut from the center; *filets mignons,* slices cut from the head end; *tournedos,* thinner and smaller slices; and *petits filets,* slices from the narrow tip of the filet.

Short Loin. From this section we get the delicious shell roasts, the portion of the loin without the tenderloin.

Sirloin Tip. This is a tender boneless cut from the tip of the sirloin, next to the top round. It is suitable for open roasting.

Round. The top round of CHOICE beef can be roasted, as can the eye of the round from PRIME beef.

Rump. Rump roasts are also cut from the round. Cuts from the rump are often sold boneless and rolled; they

Roasting Beef

Cut	Oven Temperature	Minutes per Pound			Internal Temperature
		Rare	Medium	Well Done	
Standing Rib	350°F	18	22	25	140°/160°/170°F
Rolled Rib	325°F	15	20	22	140°/160°/170°F
Shell Roast	350°F	15	18	20	140°/160°/170°F
Sirloin Tip	325°F	20	25	30	140°/160°/170°F
Tenderloin	450°F	30	(total)		140°F
Eye of the Round	375°F	15	20	25	140°/160°/170°F
Rump Roast	350°F	18	22	25	140°/160°/170°F

are most often cooked by covered roasting methods, but a rump roast of PRIME or CHOICE grade can be open-roasted.

Carving Beef

The slices of beef cool quickly after carving, so be ready to serve them immediately, or place the slices on hot plates for serving. Set the rib roast on a platter and carve according to the method you prefer.

The juices released in carving should be spooned up and added to the gravy, or, for beef *au jus*, they are spooned onto the plates without further preparation.

Boned and rolled beef can be carved by standing it on end on the dish and carving downward in slices. You may remove all the strings before carving, or snip each one as you reach it; the strings may help keep the meat firm, making it easier to carve.

Carving roast tenderloin is like carving any boned meat. Other beef cuts with bones will be easier to carve if you cut around the bones before roasting; or ask the butcher to do it.

The process of trimming a rib bone of the meat around it, which simplifies the handling of a rib roast, is called frenching. This process can be done for any bone, to provide a handle for balancing a piece of meat.

VEAL

Veal comes from young animals, slaughtered at 12 weeks for "vealers,"

up to 6 months for calves. As a result, the meat is tender and there is very little fat.

Good-quality veal is moist and fine-grained. Milk-fed veal has pale pink or off-white flesh, while the flesh of grass-fed veal is marginally darker although still pale pink. The bones are pinkish white and much softer than those of older animals. Avoid veal that looks dried up or brownish or any that has developed a bluish or mottled appearance. Veal contains little gristle and very little fat, except around the kidneys. However, there is a considerable amount of gelatinous connective tissue that dissolves during long slow cooking.

If you need veal for a specific recipe, tell your butcher how much you want and how you plan to cook it, and ask his advice.

When roasting veal, remember that it is young and lean; it must be cooked gently at low temperatures. A

meat thermometer should show an internal temperature of 170°F. If you lack a thermometer, test with a skewer; the juices should be clear, without any trace of pink. It is important to prevent drying out of veal while roasting it; without careful treatment, it can become dry and tasteless. For a traditional roast, you may try larding or barding or adding liquid to the pan, or a combination of techniques. If you bard a roast, it will be almost self-basting. However, the delicate taste of veal is better treated by brushing it with oil, since the fat used for barding or larding will give a different flavor. A small amount of liquid—½ cup of water, stock or white wine—in the bottom of the roasting pan will help prevent dryness by creating a moist atmosphere.

Stuffing a veal roast helps to keep it moist and has the additional advantage of enhancing the somewhat bland flavor. Lemon juice and rind, thyme, carrots, onions and tomatoes are good ingredients for flavoring veal.

There are only a few cuts suitable for roasting.

Shoulder. The shoulder provides an arm roast and a blade roast. Boned and rolled shoulder is good for roasting and cheaper than leg or loin. It is also suitable for pot-roasting and braising and may be purchased as boneless veal for fricassees, casseroles and stews.

Rack or Rib. This portion is considerably larger than the rack of lamb or pork, so it is an excellent choice for serving many portions. It requires more time at low temperature

Roasting Veal

Cut	Oven Temperature	Minutes per Pound	Internal Temperature
Shoulder	300°F	20 to 30	170°F
Rack or Rib	325°F	30 to 40	170°F
Breast	325°F	35 to 40	170°F
Loin	325°F	20 to 30	170°F
Round	300°F	20 to 25	170°F
Rump	325°F	25 to 30	170°F

Carving a Loin of Veal

1 Starting close to the backbone, carve with the grain. Turn the roast if necessary to complete the top side.

2 With the backbone on the fork side, carve smaller slices from the meatiest end, still carving with the grain.

3 Turn roast over to expose the flank. Carve smaller slices down to the bone, at an angle, to remove all meat.

than a beef rib. Two racks can be tied together to form a crown, a spectacular roast for a party. The rib section is often cut into chops.

Breast. Veal breast that has been boned, stuffed and rolled can be roasted in a low oven; it is also suited to pot-roasting and braising.

Loin. Veal loin is excellent for roasting, either on the bone or boned. It is often cut into loin chops.

Leg. Veal leg provides rump and round roasts. The shanks are usually sawed across the bone into 2-inch-thick pieces for *osso buco*. Veal knuckles, with their gelatin content, are an excellent addition to stocks, especially those prepared for aspics. It is the round of the leg that is cut into scallops (*escalopes* or *scaloppini*).

Carving Veal

Cuts of veal that are sold boned and rolled are simply carved downward into fairly thick slices. The texture of the meat makes it difficult to cut veal into thin slices, and in any case thin slices do not retain flavor and succulence.

Rump. The rump has a complicated bone structure that makes it hard to carve. Ask your butcher to bone this cut; or cut off one section at a time and slice it. Or carve the longest possible slices, following the shape of the bone. When the bone is cleared, turn the meat over and continue carving vertically on the other side of the bone.

Round. The round cut out of the leg is a boneless piece and simple to carve.

Loin. Loin of veal is one of the few cuts carved with the grain instead of across it. Make sure the roast stands firm by trimming the base, and turn the bone toward the fork hand. Start carving close to the backbone, turning the knife in toward the bone to release each slice as you carve. If the loin is a long one, turn the roast around to remove the meat above the backbone completely.

Rack. The rack can be carved like roast beef. However, for ease in carving both loin and rack, have the butcher bone them; the bones can be tied in place for roasting, to give the most flavor, and can be removed before carving.

PORK

Pork can be roasted both on the bone and boneless. Although it is usually considered a fatty meat, American pork is slaughtered so young and lean that there is no marbling. What may look like marbling is actually muscle tissue. Therefore moisture must be added to have succulent meat. Pork must be well cooked, but that does not mean dried out. The parasite that causes trichinosis is destroyed at 137°F; therefore pork cooked to any temperature above that is safe to eat. The internal temperature of well-cooked pork should be 170°F. Pork should always be cooked at low temperature. Because this meat is rich in flavor, it is accompanied well with acid fruits such as apples or cranberries.

Pork does not keep as well as beef. Store it under refrigeration for no longer than 3 days for large pieces, only 1 day for ground pork or small pieces.

Good-quality meat from a young animal is firm and dry, fine-grained, with a pleasant pink color. The fat should be creamy white and the rind smooth and supple. Freshly cut surfaces should be slightly moist.

If pork is to be roasted by the English method, with a crisp, browned rind called crackling, buy it with the rind on. To help the rind become crisper, score it closely and deeply. Cut right through the rind into the fat underneath, or be sure the butcher does it. Pork can be roasted without the rind. If you intend to roast that way (which is more usual in the United States), choose a rindless roast or ask the butcher to remove the rind, but be sure to take the rind home with you and cook it in the pan with the roast to enrich the gravy, or reserve it for braising other meats.

Pork may be marinated to tenderize and flavor it; be sure to use only white wine or white-wine vinegar so as not to discolor the meat. The loin and tenderloin, which have little fat, tend to dry out if open-roasted without basting or barding. Brush a little oil or butter on the surface of the roast before roasting, and baste frequently. A pork roast can also be covered for part of the roasting time, with a little wine and water or stock added to the pan.

Pork has more flavor when roasted on the bone, but it can be boned and rolled, which does make it much easier to carve. Also, a boned piece can be stuffed. Stuffing a loin or boned blade roast keeps the meat from drying so quickly during cooking. To make a hole for the stuffing, cut the meat two thirds of the way through from one end to the other along the center, keeping the meat still in one piece. If the piece is large, make 2 additional lengthwise cuts to divide each

Carving a Shoulder of Pork

1 Remove a few slices from the smaller side to form a level base. Set the roast with that side down.

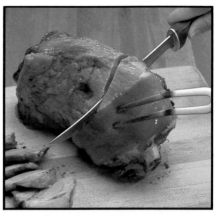

2 Hold the carving fork at the bone on the cut surface and cut down in front of the elbow joint.

side into 2 sections. Spread the stuffing over the meat, working it down into the cuts. Reshape the meat to enclose the stuffing and tie it along its length.

For a thinner piece of meat, just make a single cut and stuff it. The tenderloin can be split and reassembled around a stuffing, like a sandwich, to make a more impressive main dish.

Shoulder. The shoulder, either picnic or butt, can be roasted. These portions have bones that make carving difficult, so they are often boned and rolled for roasting.

Loin. The center loin produces the juiciest and tenderest meat, but the blade and sirloin portions are also excellent for roasting. A boneless loin is also good; this is usually rolled for roasting. The blade end is meaty and tender, although somewhat fatty. The sirloin end produces sirloin roasts. All loin roasts contain ribs that can be cut into chops.

Tenderloin. This is the tenderest portion of the pig, similar to the filet of beef. It is located underneath the sirloin. It can be roasted whole or can be split and stuffed for roasting.

Spareribs. These sections of the side are successfully cooked by oven-roasting, especially if they have been simmered first to release some of the fat.

Leg. The leg portion produces several cuts suitable for roasting—the butt half, the shank half and, for a huge roast, the whole leg.

Roasting Pork

Cut	Oven Temperature	Minutes per Pound	Internal Temperature
Shoulder	325°F	25 to 35	170°F
Loin	325°F	30 to 35	170°F
Tenderloin	325°F	45 (total)	170°F
Spareribs	325°F	25 to 30	170°F
Leg, whole	325°F	20 to 25	170°F
half	325°F	30 to 35	170°F

Add 20 to 25 minutes extra to the total time for boned or rolled cuts.

Carving Pork

Make sure the carving knife is sharp. Remove part or all of the crackling, if you have it, by sliding the knife horizontally through the layer of fat that separates crackling from meat. Cut the crackling into strips and arrange on a

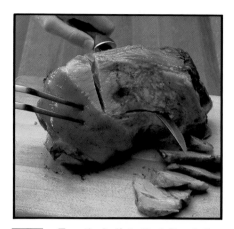

3 Turn the knife to the left and slice along the top of the arm bone.

4 Lift off the top section of the meat and slice it on the diagonal.

5 Cut off the portions on each side of the arm bone, and slice; these slices will be smaller.

small serving platter. Carve the pork into moderately thick slices. Arrange portions with some crackling and some of any stuffing.

Shoulder. This cut is much easier to deal with if it has been boned, or if it has been cooked with moist heat. If it has been roasted on the bone, cut off the top portion above the arm bone and slice it on the diagonal. Then cut off the portions on the sides of the bone and slice in the same manner.

Loin. If the loin has been prepared for roasting by removal of the chine bone and by cracking of the backbone between the chops, it is easier to cut into chop portions.

Tenderloin. This is cut into fairly thick slices just like a filet of beef.

Spareribs. These are simply cut apart into portions of 1, 2, or 3 bones; cut portions with a single bone for eating in hand at picnics. If it is difficult to cut with a carving knife, you may help things along with poultry shears.

Leg. To carve a leg with its bones, cut down to the bone just inside the shank joint. Then cut horizontally along the leg bone to cut off the layer of meat on top. Transfer that piece of meat to a separate platter and slice at an angle. Then separate the leg bone at both ends and lift it out. Carve the lower

portion of the meat in the same fashion as the top part. If you are carving half of a leg, follow the same process. The meat around the shank bone will require careful cutting with a boning knife, and the slices will not be so large or even.

A boned leg is carved like any boneless roast.

LAMB

All cuts of lamb suitable for roasting will be tender and flavorful. Lamb is at its best in spring or early summer when just a few months old. Frozen lamb brings "spring lamb" to markets out of season. The natural flavor of young, top-quality lamb is delicious.

Lamb that is slaughtered at a year or older is mutton, and tougher and fatter; meat from these older animals seldom appears in our markets. If in doubt about the age of lamb in your shop, choose smaller cuts. Fresh spring lamb is pale pink in color and lightly marbled with fat whereas older meat is redder and fattier. This pinkness is not seen in meat that has been frozen. The fat of young lamb is firm and white but not brittle. The outer layer of papery skin, the fell, should be

smooth and supple. When choosing legs and shoulders, pick those that are thick and well rounded rather than scrawny. A thin covering of fat is essential for good flavor; even if you don't like to eat the fat, roast the meat complete and trim away the fat after cooking.

Basting is usually unnecessary for lamb, nor do you need to brush the roast with oil or add drippings before cooking unless the skin has been removed or the meat has a large cut surface that needs to be kept moist.

Shoulder. The shoulder has a higher proportion of fat and bone than other roasting cuts, but the meat is sweet and succulent; the weight may range from 4 to 6 pounds. Small shoulders are usually roasted whole, but larger shoulders can be cut into two smaller roasts, the blade and the arm roasts. However, any lamb shoulder will make a better roast after boning, prepared either flat or rolled. Shoulder is usually cheaper than leg or loin.

Rack or Rib. The rack is both sections of the rib chops, often cut into chops instead of being sold as one piece. A half rack is a small rib roast. The layer of meat is thin and it needs only brief cooking. Both racks can be used to make a crown roast.

Loin. This is a cut from one side

Roasting Lamb

Cut	Oven Temperature	Minutes per Pound	Internal Temperature
Shoulder	325°F	20 to 25	145°F
Rack or Rib	350°F	40 to 45 total	145°F
Loin	350°F	40 to 45 total	145°F
Saddle	325°F	15 to 18	145°F
Leg	350°F	15	145°F

The internal temperature is for medium-rare lamb. If you prefer it well done, roast all cuts at 325°F and set the meat thermometer at your preferred temperature—160° or 170°F. However, the rack and loin are best roasted to medium-rare.

of the back between the leg and the rack, weighing from 3 to 4 pounds. The butcher normally cuts off about 2 inches of the belly flap and removes excess fat from inside the loin. Ask the butcher to remove the chine bone or cut between the chops to facilitate carving. The roast can be skinned and the fat scored for a decorative appearance. Always remove the skin if you plan to baste or glaze the loin. This cut can also be boned completely and can be stuffed and rolled.

Saddle. The saddle is a double loin roast, weighing 6 to 8 pounds. You will get a better yield from a large sad-

Roasting Leg of Lamb

1 Have the butcher crack 3 chops at the sirloin end and french the end of the shank bone.

2 Let the lamb reach room temperature, about 1 hour. Preheat oven to 350°F.

3 Cut garlic cloves into thin slivers and separate individual fresh rosemary leaves.

4 Make tiny incisions through the skin of the lamb and insert garlic slivers and rosemary leaves.

5 Put extra pieces of garlic and sprigs of rosemary underneath the roast.

6 Roast lamb for 15 minutes per pound for medium-rare, or to 145°F on the meat thermometer.

Carving Roast Leg of Lamb

dle, as there is a high proportion of bone. Choose a thick, compact saddle. Have the butcher prepare the saddle for the oven; the whole piece should be skinned, and the fat scored in a diamond pattern. The sides, called the aprons, are folded under and the whole piece is tied securely in shape.

Leg. The leg is a lean cut, weighing 5 to 8 pounds. Only rarely does one find a leg of lamb weighing less than 5 pounds. The butcher normally chops the knuckle bone, sometimes leaving it attached by the skin only so that it can be removed easily after roasting. The thin skin covering the leg is usually left on and helps to retain all the meat juices. Basting is unnecessary for a whole leg. However, when cooking the sirloin end of a leg, which has two cut surfaces, basting is essential. The shank end tends to be muscular; it can be open-roasted, but it is often cooked by a moist-heat method. The leg can also be boned completely.

Carving Lamb

Carve lamb in slices no thinner than ¼ inch, for best flavor and succulence.

Shoulder. To carve a shoulder on the bone is difficult for a nonprofessional. It is better to have this cut boned before roasting. It is then carved like any boneless cut.

Rack or Rib. This cut is usually prepared by the butcher to aid carving. The chine bone is removed, or the backbone is cut between the chops. When the rack is well prepared, it is simple to carve it; just cut between the rib bones to divide it into thick chops. The rack can be boned completely before roasting, with the bones tied to the meat to add flavor.

Loin. Like the rack, this cut can be chopped through the backbone between the ribs. To carve, simply cut between the rib bones, dividing the meat into thick chops.

Saddle. A saddle is carved differently from the single loin, even though it is two loins still together. The

1 Cut off the cracked chops at the sirloin end.

2 Protecting your hand with paper toweling, hold end of frenched shank bone to keep roast steady and cut down just inside shank joint.

3 Continue to cut diagonal slices toward the leg bone. Then slide knife under slices to release them.

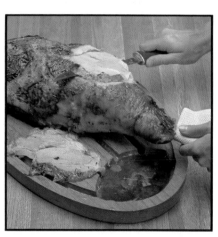

OR Hold shank bone and slice meat lengthwise down the leg.

meat is entirely freed from the backbone and ribs before being carved. Then it is not sliced into choplike portions but is carved across the top, slightly on the diagonal, into long thin pieces. Because of the bones, vertical slicing gives raggedy pieces.

Leg. To carve a leg on the bone, first crack the chops at the sirloin end and trim the shank bone to use it as a

handle. Cut off the chops, then slice toward the leg bone, cutting on a slant toward the shank end. When this side is carved, turn the leg over and carve the smaller side in the same fashion. A boned roast is carved like any boneless cut, carving slightly on the diagonal. If you have only a shank or sirloin end, carve either like the same portion of the whole leg.

Filet of Beef with Madeira Sauce

8 portions

4	tablespoons butter		½	cup Madeira wine
1	tablespoon oil		1	cup Demi-Glace Sauce
4	pounds filet of beef			(see Volume 3 Index)
4	ounces unsalted pork			salt and pepper
	fatback or beef fat from			
	the flank			

Preheat oven to 450°F. Put the butter and oil in the roasting pan and put the pan in the oven. Stud the top of the filet with larding strips cut from the fatback or the beef fat *(piquer)*. Remove the pan from the oven. Set the beef on a rack and the rack in the roasting pan. Baste the top of the meat with the hot butter and oil. Return the pan to the oven and roast the filet for 30 minutes, basting it once halfway through the cooking time. After 30 minutes the meat should be rare, or 140°F on a meat thermometer. If you like it more done, cook it for 10 minutes longer, to 160°F. If you test the meat with a skewer, the juices should be rosy but not red for rare. On no account overcook this cut of meat.

Transfer the beef to a warmed serving platter and let it rest for 15 minutes before carving it.

Make the sauce: Skim off excess fat from the pan juices. Add the Madeira and boil for about 5 minutes, until the liquid has reduced by half. Stir around the pan to release any meat juices and deglaze it. Add the demi-glace sauce to the pan and boil for 5 minutes longer, stirring all the time. Strain the sauce into a sauceboat. Remove strings from the beef and carve into 1-inch-thick slices.

Serve with steamed new potatoes, tossed in butter and sprinkled with paprika, watercress bouquets, and whole mushrooms sautéed in butter.

English Roast Beef

6 portions

4 tablespoons oil
2 pounds potatoes
1 3-rib roast of beef, about 5 pounds
   salt and black pepper

1 slice of tomato
1 teaspoon sugar
½ cup vegetable cooking water or light stock
½ cup red wine

Preheat oven to 425°F. Pour the oil into the roasting pan and put the pan in the oven. Peel the potatoes; if they are too large to roast whole, cut them into halves or quarters. Take the pan out of the oven and put in the potatoes, spooning the hot oil over them. Arrange a rack over the potatoes. Place beef on the rack, fat side up. If you are using a meat thermometer, insert it into the thickest part of the meat, not touching bone or fat. Roast the beef for 1 hour.

Remove pan from the oven, remove the rack and the meat, and turn all the potatoes over with tongs. Baste the potatoes, then salt them lightly for a crisp finish. Replace the rack and the beef and baste the beef with some of the hot oil and pan juices. Roast the beef for 30 minutes longer. The internal temperature should be 140°F for rare. Transfer beef

to a warmed serving platter or a carving board. Use tongs to transfer potatoes to surround the beef. Keep everything hot while you make gravy.

Pour off the fat in the roasting pan until the meat juices start to flow out, then skim off more fat with a spoon. Add the tomato slice with the sugar sprinkled on it. Place the pan over moderate heat on top of the stove and cook until the sugar turns dark brown. Add the vegetable water or stock and the wine. Boil for 10 minutes, until liquid is reduced and the gravy is slightly thickened. Taste for seasoning; the gravy will not need salt, since the salt from the potatoes will be in the meat juices. Strain gravy into a sauceboat and serve with the roast and the potatoes.

Roast Beef with Sauce Diable

6 portions

3 pounds top round of beef

3 tablespoons oil

Sauce Diable

3 large shallots
¾ cup red wine
1 tablespoon red-wine vinegar
1 cup brown stock
2 tablespoons red-currant jelly

2 teaspoons prepared Dijon-style mustard
2 teaspoons prepared horseradish
1 teaspoon Worcestershire sauce
   salt and black pepper

Use only PRIME or CHOICE for this recipe; other grades are better braised or roasted by the covered method. Preheat oven to 350°F. Pour the oil into the baking pan and heat it in the oven. Remove pan from oven, put in a rack, and place the meat on the rack. Baste the beef with the hot oil in the pan. Return pan to the oven and roast for 1¼ hours. Baste the beef at 30-minute intervals.

Peel and chop the shallots. Assemble the other ingredients for the sauce. Test the meat with a skewer; the juices should be rosy; or if you have used a meat thermometer, the internal temperature should be 160°F for medium-rare.

Pour off the fat from the roasting pan, then skim off

more fat with a spoon. Add the chopped shallots to the pan and cook over moderate heat until shallots are soft and translucent. Stir occasionally with a wooden spoon. Pour in the wine and vinegar and boil for 10 minutes, until the liquids are reduced to about ¼ cup. Add brown stock and currant jelly and continue to simmer. Stir with a wooden spoon until jelly is dissolved. Add the mustard, horseradish, Worcestershire and seasoning to taste. Strain the sauce into a warmed sauceboat and serve with the beef. Alternatively, the meat may be carved into slices and some of the sauce may be used to coat the slices.

Breast of Veal with Anchovy and Herb Stuffing

6 portions

4½ pounds breast of veal, unboned
2 tablespoons butter

1 tablespoon oil
2 tablespoons flour
1 cup light veal stock

Anchovy and Herb Stuffing

2 slices of smoked bacon
1½ ounces suet
4 shallots
6 anchovy fillets
1¼ cups fresh white bread crumbs
1 tablespoon minced parsley

1 tablespoon snipped chives
1 teaspoon minced thyme, or
  ½ teaspoon dried
salt and pepper
½ lemon
1 large egg

Have the butcher cut a pocket along one side of the meat above the bones. Ask him to cut through the sternum bone at intervals to aid carving.

Make the stuffing: Chop the bacon and shred the suet. Peel and mince the shallots. Cut anchovy fillets into very small pieces. Mix the bread crumbs with the bacon, suet, shallots, anchovies and herbs, and season the mixture well. Grate the lemon rind and squeeze the lemon half. Beat the egg and combine egg, lemon rind and juice with the dry stuffing ingredients. Moisten the stuffing with stock, adding it 1 tablespoon at a time, until the stuffing holds together. Do not let the mixture become too wet.

Preheat oven to 325°F. Wipe the meat with a clean damp cloth. Using a tablespoon, pack the stuffing into the pocket above the bones, pushing it in well. Skewer the open-ing and tie around the skewers with string. Put the butter and oil in the roasting pan and heat in the oven. Place the veal on a rack, pocket side up, and place the rack in the pan. Baste the veal with some of the hot butter from the bottom of the pan. Place the pan in the oven and roast for about 2½ hours, basting at 20-minute intervals throughout.

When veal is done, transfer it to a warmed carving platter. Pour off the fat in the roasting pan. Stir in the flour and cook for 1 minute, stirring to mix flour into pan drippings. Add the remaining stock, bring to a boil, and simmer for 3 minutes. Check seasoning and pour the gravy into a warmed sauceboat. Carve the breast in strips between the bones to give each person a bone and a portion of stuffing with the meat above.

Roast Shoulder of Veal with Stuffing Balls

6 portions

4½ to 5 pounds boneless shoulder of veal
5 ounces unsalted pork fatback or unsmoked bacon
2 tablespoons butter
1½ cups veal stock

3 to 4 cups stuffing, such as Bacon and Celery Stuffing (see Volume 2 Index)
6 tablespoons flour
1 tablespoon oil
2 tablespoons cream

Preheat oven to 325°F. Wipe the meat with a clean damp cloth. Cut the pork fat into thin slices. Melt the butter and brush the top of the veal, then lay the pork fat slices on top, to cover the whole upper surface. Place the meat on a rack in the roasting pan. Pour ½ cup of the stock into the pan. Put the pan in the center of the oven and roast the veal for 20 minutes per pound.

Meanwhile make the stuffing; shape it into 1-inch balls and roll them in 2 tablespoons of the flour to coat them all over. Pour the oil into a baking dish and place in the oven to heat. Add the stuffing balls to the hot oil and turn them with a perforated spoon to coat them with oil. Bake the stuffing balls for 1 hour.

About 30 minutes before the veal should be done, remove the slices of fat on the top. Sprinkle the surface evenly with 2 tablespoons flour. Baste with the juices from the pan and return to the oven. At the end of the cooking time, remove veal from the oven. The temperature should be 170°F. If you lack a thermometer, test the meat with a skewer; the juices should be colorless. Transfer the veal to a large serving platter and surround it with the stuffing balls.

Make gravy with the pan juices. First pour off as much of the fat as possible, then spoon off more. Mix remaining 2 tablespoons flour with 4 tablespoons stock and stir it into the pan juices. Simmer the mixture, stirring, until it thickens; add more of the stock if needed. Season the gravy, then stir in the cream. Strain the gravy into a sauceboat and serve with the veal.

Applesauce

makes about 2 cups

1	pound cooking apples	4	tablespoons sugar
1	strip of lemon or orange peel	1	tablespoon butter

Peel, core, and slice the apples. Work quickly to prevent discoloring. Drop apples into a stainless-steel saucepan; add the lemon or orange peel, 2 tablespoons water, and 2 tablespoons of the sugar. Cover the pan and stew apples gently for 10 minutes, until tender. Taste, and add the rest of the sugar if needed. For a rough-textured sauce, beat the apples with a wire whisk or a potato masher. For a smooth sauce,

purée the apples in a blender or food processor, or press the apples through a food mill.

Return sauce to the pan. Taste again and add more sugar if needed. If the sauce is thin, simmer it uncovered until it reaches the desired consistency. Stir in the butter. Serve hot or cold, with pork.

Roast Loin of Pork, French Style

6 portions

1	blade loin of pork, about 4 pounds	½	cup white wine
2	large garlic cloves	½	cup stock
6	sprigs of rosemary or thyme		salt and black pepper

Have the butcher remove the rind and chine bone; keep both rind and bone to enrich gravy. Wipe the meat with a damp cloth. Peel garlic cloves, cut into slivers, and tuck the slivers in between the bones. Put the pork in a ceramic or glass container just large enough to hold it. Put 2 sprigs of rosemary in the container and pour in the wine and ½ cup water. Turn the meat to moisten all sides, cover, and refrigerate for 2 hours.

Preheat oven to 325°F. Put the pork rind, chine bone and 2 rosemary sprigs in the bottom of a roasting pan.

Remove pork from marinade and insert a meat thermometer into the meat, not touching bone or fat. Put the pork on a rack and set it in the roasting pan. Pour in the wine marinade. Roast the pork in the center of the oven for about 2 hours. The internal temperature should be approaching 170°F. Lift the meat to a warmed serving plate. Remove rind and bone from the pan. Spoon off as much fat as possible. Pour in the stock, bring to a boil, and simmer for 3 minutes. Check the seasoning. Strain the gravy into a sauceboat. Garnish the top of the meat with the remaining sprigs of fresh herbs.

Roast Loin of Pork with Cranberry Apples

6 portions

4	pounds center loin of pork	5	tablespoons sugar
1	tablespoon oil	5	tablespoons butter
6	medium-size cooking apples	1	cup cranberry sauce, homemade or canned

Preheat oven to 325°F. Wipe the meat with a clean damp cloth. Brush the oil over the top of the meat. Place the pork on a rack in a roasting pan large enough to hold it. Roast the meat in the center of the oven for 2 hours. The internal temperature should be 170°F. If the pork seems to be drying too much, brush it with more oil every 30 minutes.

Meanwhile, wash and core the apples and run the tip of a knife around the center of each one, just cutting through the skin, so the apples cook without bursting. Butter a baking

dish and place apples side by side in it. Divide the sugar and remaining butter among the apples, spooning it into the core holes. Pour a little water in the dish around the apples. About 1 hour before the meat should be done, put the dish of apples on the rack below the meat. About 5 minutes before the meat is done, warm the cranberry sauce in a small saucepan with 1 tablespoon water.

Transfer the pork to a warmed serving platter. Carefully drain the apples and arrange them around the meat. Put a large spoonful of cranberry sauce into each apple and over them. Serve the roast at once.

If you wish to serve gravy, make pan gravy with the pan juices, a little flour for thickening, and some stock.

Variation: If you have large apples, they can be halved across and baked. Spoon cranberry sauce across the cut surfaces and into the cores for serving.

Loin of Pork with Juniper Berries

6 to 8 portions

1 loin of pork, 5 to 6 pounds	¼ teaspoon black pepper
2 garlic cloves	1¼ cups beef stock
12 · juniper berries	¾ cup dry white wine
½ teaspoon salt	

Have the butcher bone the loin and trim off excess fat. The oven-ready piece should weigh about 4 pounds. Unroll it to prepare for roasting.

Preheat oven to 325°F. Peel garlic cloves and cut into thin slices. Make small incisions in the pork and insert garlic slices. Crush the juniper berries with salt and pepper in a small mortar. Sprinkle the juniper mixture over the meat, roll it up, and tie it securely with white string. Put the pork on a rack in a roasting pan and roast for 35 minutes per pound, until the juices are clear when the meat is pierced with a thin skewer. The internal temperature should be 170°F. Use a large fork, or 2 forks, to lift the pork to a large sheet of aluminum foil; wrap the foil around the pork and return it to the oven to keep hot.

Pour off the fat from the roasting pan. Use a wooden spoon to scrape up any brown bits on the bottom and sides. Add the stock and the wine and place the roasting pan over moderate heat. Bring liquids to a boil, reduce heat to low, and simmer for 8 to 10 minutes, until the sauce is somewhat reduced. Pour sauce into a warmed sauceboat. Remove pork from its foil wrapping and remove all the strings. Slice pork and place on a heated serving dish; serve with the sauce.

Chinese Roast Pork

4 portions

Marinade

1½	tablespoons soy sauce
1	tablespoon hoisin sauce
½	teaspoon salt
1½	tablespoons peanut oil
1	tablespoon soft brown sugar
2	pork tenderloins, each about 12 ounces
1	piece of fresh gingerroot, ½ inch thick
2	garlic cloves

4	ounces carrots
4	ounces cauliflower
5	ounces broccoli
6	tablespoons oil
1½	teaspoons salt
	freshly ground black pepper
½	teaspoon chili powder
1	teaspoon sugar
5	teaspoons soy sauce
1½	cups chicken stock
1	teaspoon sesame oil
1	teaspoon cornstarch

Combine the marinade ingredients and mix well. Remove any pieces of membrane from the pork tenderloins and coat tenderloins with the marinade. Leave in the refrigerator for 3 to 4 hours, turning the tenderloins every 30 minutes to moisten all sides.

Peel and chop the gingerroot and garlic. Scrub and scrape the carrots and cut into thin slices. Wash the cauliflower and broccoli and separate into small florets. Peel any tough stems of broccoli and cauliflower and cut into thin slices.

Preheat oven to 400°F. Arrange the pork tenderloins on a rack in the roasting pan and spoon 1 tablespoon of the oil over the base of the pan. Roast the pork for 30 minutes, turning once. After 15 minutes begin cooking the vegetables. Pour 2 tablespoons of the oil into a wok or large deep skillet with a lid. Add the chopped gingerroot and half of the garlic and stir over high heat for a few seconds. Add carrot slices and stir-fry for 2 minutes. Sprinkle with ½ teaspoon of the salt and black pepper to taste. Push the carrots to one side of the wok. Add 1½ tablespoons oil and remaining garlic.

When hot, add cauliflower and stir-fry for 2 minutes. Sprinkle with ½ teaspoon of the salt and the chili powder and push to the other side of the pan. Heat remaining 1½ tablespoons oil in the center of the wok, add the broccoli, and stir-fry for 1½ minutes. Sprinkle with the sugar and 2 teaspoons of the soy sauce, and stir for a few seconds. Pour ½ cup of the stock gently over each pile of vegetables. Cover the wok and simmer over lowered heat for 4 minutes. Uncover and pour ¼ cup stock and the sesame oil over the vegetables and stir gently. Arrange the vegetables in groups around a warmed serving platter.

Remove pork from the oven and cut across the grain into thin slices. Arrange the slices overlapping in the center of the vegetables. Keep everything warm. Mix 1 teaspoon cornstarch with 1 tablespoon of the stock. Add remaining stock and 3 teaspoons soy sauce to the wok and stir well. Add the cornstarch mixture, stirring all the time, and bring to a boil. Simmer until the sauce is thickened and clear, about 1 minute. Serve the sauce separately.

Loin of Pork with Oranges and Pineapple

6 to 8 portions

1	loin of pork, 5 to 6 pounds

Marinade

1	1-inch piece of gingerroot
1	teaspoon whole coriander berries
1	teaspoon black peppercorns
2	garlic cloves
½	teaspoon ground allspice

1	teaspoon prepared Dijon-style mustard
1	teaspoon salt
	grated rind of 1 orange
5	tablespoons soy sauce
¼	cup fresh lemon juice
2	tablespoons vegetable oil
2	large oranges
1	small pineapple
2	pounds potatoes

Have the butcher bone the loin of pork, trim off excess fat, and roll and tie the meat. The oven-ready piece should weigh about 4 pounds.

Make the marinade: Peel and grate the gingerroot. Crush the coriander berries and black peppercorns in a mortar. Peel garlic cloves and put through a press. Combine garlic with allspice, mustard, salt, orange rind, soy sauce and lemon juice. Place the pork in a ceramic or glass container that will just hold it, and pour the marinade over it. Marinate pork in a cool place for 3 hours, turning the meat frequently to moisten it all over.

Preheat oven to 325°F. Remove pork from the marinade. Pour the marinade into a small saucepan and bring to a boil. Remove saucepan from heat. Spoon the oil into a large roasting pan and place it in the oven. When oil is hot, put in the pork, fat side up. Roast the pork for 2¼ hours, until the juices are clear when the meat is pierced with a skewer. The internal temperature should be 170°F. Baste the pork every 30 minutes with the marinade.

Meanwhile, peel the oranges and cut into thick slices. Peel the pineapple, core it, and cut into chunks. Peel and cube the potatoes, cover with boiling water, and simmer for 10 minutes. Drain potatoes, rinse with cold water, and drain again. About 45 minutes before the pork should be cooked, cover the meat with orange slices and add pineapple chunks and potato cubes to the roasting pan. After 25 minutes, remove the pan from the oven and turn the potatoes over. Return to the oven to finish roasting.

When the pork is done, transfer it to a carving board. Return the orange slices to the roasting pan and put back in the oven. Carve the pork into thick slices and arrange them on a serving platter. Spoon the hot fruit over the pork and arrange the potatoes alongside. Remove excess fat from the cooking juices and strain the juices over the pork. Serve immediately.

Roast Fresh Pork with Cream and Wine Sauce

6 portions

3 tablespoons olive oil
2 tablespoons lemon juice
1 teaspoon salt
½ teaspoon black pepper
1 teaspoon dried sage
1 tablespoon chopped fresh
   parsley
1 leg of fresh pork, 5 pounds
2 garlic cloves

Cream and Wine Sauce

1 teaspoon cornstarch
1 cup plus 1 tablespoon dry
   white wine
1 teaspoon dried sage
½ cup heavy cream

Preheat oven to 325°F. In a small mixing bowl combine the olive oil, lemon juice, salt, pepper, sage and parsley. With a sharp knife make 4 incisions in the pork. Peel and halve the garlic cloves and insert the pieces in the incisions. Rub the meat with the olive-oil mixture and set aside for 10 minutes.

Place the pork on a rack in a roasting pan and roast for 2½ hours, until the pork reaches the internal temperature of 170°F, or test the meat by piercing it with a thin skewer; the juices should be colorless. Remove pork from the oven.

Make the sauce: Dissolve the cornstarch in 1 tablespoon of the wine. Pour remaining wine into a small saucepan and bring to a boil over moderate heat. Stir in the cornstarch mixture and the sage, stirring constantly. Cook for 3 minutes, until the sauce has thickened. Reduce heat to low and gradually stir in the cream. Cook the sauce gently until it is hot, but do not let it boil. Pour the sauce into a warmed sauceboat and serve with the pork.

Spareribs Marinated with Herbs and Spices

4 portions

3 pounds pork spareribs
1 large bay leaf
1 tablespoon dried sage
1½ teaspoons grated nutmeg

¼ teaspoon ground allspice
½ teaspoon freshly ground
   black pepper

Have the sheet of spareribs cracked to make later carving easier. Wipe the meat with a damp cloth. Make the marinade: Crumble the bay leaf into a bowl and add sage, nutmeg, allspice and pepper. Mix well. Sprinkle the marinade over both surfaces of the meat and rub in thoroughly with your fingers. Continue until all surfaces have been covered and all the marinade has been used. Put the meat on a rack standing on a plate or tray or a large sheet of foil. Cover loosely with foil or plastic wrap and refrigerate for 24 hours.

Preheat oven to 325°F. Put a rack in the bottom of a large roasting pan and place the meat, fat side up, on the rack. Roast the ribs in the center of the oven for 1½ hours. Check that the pork is cooked by piercing it with a skewer in the meatiest part; the juices should be colorless. Transfer spareribs to a hot serving dish. Cut the ribs into portions and serve with a sweet and pungent sauce or with a barbecue sauce.

Mint Sauce

makes about ½ cup

3 tablespoons minced fresh
   mint

1 tablespoon soft brown
   sugar
¼ cup white-wine vinegar

Put mint and sugar in a small saucepan. Add 2 tablespoons boiling water and stir until the sugar is dissolved and the mint colors the water. Stir in the vinegar and set aside until cold.

Make this sauce about 2 hours before it is needed, to allow all the flavor to develop. Serve with roast lamb.

Rack of Lamb with Currant and Orange Glaze

4 portions

1 rack of lamb, 3 pounds	1 tablespoon orange juice
2 tablespoons red-currant jelly	2 teaspoons lemon juice
	salt and pepper

Have the butcher cut off the tops of the rib bones, remove the chine bone, and crack the bones at the joints.

Preheat oven to 350°F. Place the meat, fat side up, on a rack in a roasting pan. Lay the cut-off bones in the bottom of the pan to enrich the gravy. Roast the meat for 25 minutes. Meanwhile, melt the jelly in the orange juice in a small saucepan. Remove pan from the oven and spoon the jelly and orange mixture over the fat side of the meat. Continue roasting for 20 minutes longer for rare or 30 minutes for well done. The internal temperature for rare should be 145°F. Transfer the meat to a warmed serving dish and keep it warm.

Pour off the fat in the roasting pan, stir in the lemon juice, and bring to a boil, stirring. Cook over moderate heat for 3 minutes. Season to taste and serve very hot; there will be only a few spoonfuls of the sauce.

Roast Leg of Lamb with Provençal Sauce

6 to 8 portions

1	leg of lamb, 5 to 6 pounds	½	teaspoon salt
6	slices of lean bacon	½	teaspoon black pepper
2	garlic cloves	1	bouquet garni (4 parsley
2	tablespoons butter		sprigs, 2 thyme sprigs, 1
2	cups cooked rice		bay leaf, tied together)
2	tablespoons chopped fresh	¾	cup dry red wine
	parsley	½	cup beef stock

Provençal Sauce

2	eggplants, each 1½ pounds	1¾	cups canned peeled tomatoes
1	large green pepper	½	teaspoon salt
2	garlic cloves	½	teaspoon black pepper
¾	cup olive oil		

Have the butcher bone the leg of lamb; the boned meat should weigh about 4 pounds. Preheat oven to 350°F. Lay the meat out flat on a board. Chop the bacon. Peel the garlic cloves and put through a press. Melt the butter in a medium-size frying pan over moderate heat. Add the bacon pieces and cook, stirring occasionally, for 5 minutes, until bacon is crisp and brown. Stir in the rice, parsley, puréed garlic, salt and pepper. Cook the mixture, stirring, for 3 minutes. Remove pan from heat. Spread the stuffing mixture evenly over the lamb. Roll up the meat, jelly-roll fashion, and secure it with white string.

Place the *bouquet garni* on the bottom of a large roasting pan and set the lamb on top. Heat the wine and beef stock together over moderate heat until the mixture comes to a boil. Pour the mixture around the lamb. Place the lamb in the oven and roast, basting occasionally, for 1 hour, until the lamb is cooked. The internal temperature should be 145°F. If you test the meat with a skewer, the juices that run out should be faintly rosy.

Meanwhile make the sauce: Cut the eggplants into small cubes and soak them in salted water for 30 minutes. Drain and dry them thoroughly on paper towels. Wash and halve the green pepper, discard stem, seeds and ribs, and chop the pepper. Peel the garlic cloves and put through a press. Heat the oil in a large frying pan over moderate heat. When hot, add eggplant cubes and sauté them, turning to brown all sides, for 8 to 10 minutes, until they are tender. Add the chopped green pepper, puréed garlic, tomatoes with the can liquid, the salt and pepper. Cook the mixture, stirring occasionally, for 10 minutes, until it is thick and somewhat pulpy. Pour the sauce into a warmed serving bowl. Remove lamb from the oven and transfer to a warmed platter. Remove strings and carve. Serve lamb with the sauce.

Herb-Stuffed Leg of Lamb

6 portions

1	leg of lamb, 5 pounds	1	teaspoon dried thyme
6	green onions (scallions)	1	teaspoon dried basil
1	garlic clove	½	teaspoon salt
4	ounces cooked ham	¼	teaspoon black pepper
4	tablespoons chopped fresh parsley	1	tablespoon lemon juice

Have the butcher bone the leg of lamb. Preheat oven to 350°F. Lay the meat out flat on a board. Wash and chop the green onions. Peel the garlic and put through a press. Chop the ham. In a mixing bowl combine the green onions, garlic, ham, parsley, thyme, basil, salt, pepper and lemon juice. Mix with a fork. Spread the stuffing over the meat. Roll up the meat, jelly-roll fashion, and tie it with white string.

Place the lamb on a rack in a roasting pan and place it in the oven. Roast for 1¼ hours, until the meat is tender and the juices only faintly rosy when the meat is tested with a skewer. The internal temperature should be 145°F. If you prefer it well done, roast for 30 minutes longer, to 160°F. Transfer the lamb to a warmed serving platter and serve at once.

Shoulder of Lamb Boulangère

*Boulangère means "in the style of the baker's wife" and
dishes with this name are always prepared with potatoes.*

6 portions

3½	pounds lean lamb shoulder			salt and black pepper
2	large garlic cloves		1	cup brown stock
8	ounces onions			chopped fresh
2	tablespoons butter			herbs—parsley,
1	tablespoon oil			watercress, chives
2	pounds potatoes			

Preheat oven to 325°F. Prepare the shoulder of lamb for roasting; do not skin it, but make incisions in the top of the meat. Peel garlic, cut into slivers, and insert the slivers in the incisions; also tuck them around the bone and flaps of skin. Peel the onions and cut into thin slices. Heat butter and oil in a skillet and sauté the onion slices until softened. Peel the potatoes and cut into thin slices.

Lightly butter a large ovenproof dish, preferably one that can be used for serving. Arrange the potato and onion slices in layers, seasoning lightly between the layers and filling the base of the dish. Pour in the stock, which should reach almost to the top of the vegetables. Arrange the lamb on top of the vegetable base. Roast the lamb in the center of the oven for 1 hour and 20 minutes for medium rare, 2 hours for well done. The internal temperature for medium rare should be 145°F, for well done it should be 160° to 170°F. Sprinkle the potatoes with the chopped herbs, and serve from the baking dish.

Leg of Lamb Marinated in Red Wine

4 to 6 portions

1	leg of lamb, 5 pounds	1	bouquet garni (4 parsley
5	cups red wine		sprigs, 2 thyme sprigs, 1
1¼	cups red-wine vinegar		bay leaf, tied together)
¼	cup olive oil	2	tablespoons butter
2	garlic cloves	1	tablespoon vegetable oil
1	teaspoon salt	1	tablespoon flour
½	teaspoon black pepper	¼	cup heavy cream

Place the lamb in a deep ceramic or glass container just large enough to hold it. Pour in the red wine, vinegar and olive oil. Peel the garlic and put through a press into the liquid, then add salt and pepper and stir until salt is dissolved. Add the *bouquet garni*. Turn the lamb in the mixture to be sure it is coated on all sides. Marinate the lamb for 24 hours in the refrigerator, turning and basting it every 3 or 4 hours.

Remove lamb from the marinade and place it on a rack. Let it drain for 20 minutes. Reserve the marinade. Preheat oven to 450°F. Dry the lamb with paper towels and place the rack in a roasting pan.

Melt the butter with the oil in a small saucepan and pour the mixture over the lamb. Place the roasting pan in the oven and roast the lamb for 30 minutes. Reduce oven temperature to 350°F and roast for ¾ hour longer, basting frequently, until the juices are slightly pink when the meat is pierced with a skewer. The internal temperature should be 145°F. If you like lamb well done, roast it for 30 minutes longer, until the internal temperature is 170°F.

Remove lamb from the oven and place it on a carving board. Keep it hot. Strain 2 tablespoons of the hot fat from the roasting pan into a saucepan. With a wooden spoon, stir in the flour to make a smooth paste. Over moderate heat cook, stirring, for 2 minutes. Stir 1¼ cups of the reserved marinade into the roux. Return pan to heat and bring the sauce to a boil, stirring constantly. Cook for 2 to 3 minutes, until the sauce is thick and smooth. Reduce heat to low and stir in the cream. Cook for about 3 minutes longer. Pour the sauce into a warmed sauceboat. Serve it with the carved lamb.

Roast Leg of Lamb Coated with Mustard

6 portions

½	cup prepared Dijon-style	1	tablespoon olive oil
	mustard	1	teaspoon salt
3	tablespoons soy sauce	½	teaspoon black pepper
2	teaspoons dried rosemary	1	leg of lamb, 5 pounds
2	garlic cloves		

Preheat oven to 350°F. In a mixing bowl combine the mustard, soy sauce and rosemary. Peel garlic cloves and put through a press into the mustard mixture. With a wooden spoon gradually beat in the oil. Season with salt and pepper.

Place the lamb on a rack in a roasting pan. Use a pastry brush to coat the lamb all over with the mustard mixture. Place lamb in the oven and roast it for 1¼ hours, basting frequently, until the juices that run out are faintly rosy when the meat is tested with a skewer. The internal temperature should be 145°F. If you prefer the lamb well done, roast it for 20 minutes longer. Remove lamb from the oven and serve at once.

Variation: The mustard mixture can also be used for lamb shoulder.

Spicy Rolled Roast Lamb

6 portions

1	loin of lamb, 4 pounds		salt and black pepper
4	large garlic cloves	2	tablespoons butter
1	tablespoon ground	1	cup dry white wine
	coriander		watercress

Have the butcher bone the lamb, but be sure he gives you the bones, as they will add flavor to the roast or can be used to make broth. The oven-ready lamb should weigh about 3 pounds.

Preheat oven to 350°F. Peel and crush garlic cloves and sprinkle with the coriander. Spread this mixture over the inside of the boned meat and season it well with salt and pepper. Roll up the lamb and tie it securely with white string. Put the meat in a roasting pan, spread it with the butter, and pour in the wine. Roast the lamb for 45 minutes, basting occasionally with the wine. The internal temperature should be 145°F. If you prefer your lamb well done, cook until the internal temperature is 170°F.

Remove lamb to a serving dish, cut away the strings, and keep the lamb hot. Skim fat from the juices in the pan and boil rapidly to reduce them. Check the seasoning and pour pan juices into a sauceboat. Serve the lamb garnished with watercress.

Parslied Loin of Lamb

6 portions

4	pounds loin of lamb		¾	cup fresh white bread crumbs
1	garlic clove		3	tablespoons minced fresh parsley
5	tablespoons butter		1	teaspoon salt
1	lemon		½	teaspoon black pepper

Preheat oven to 350°F. Wipe the meat with a clean damp cloth. Halve the garlic clove and rub the cut sides liberally over the underside and cut surfaces of the meat. Cut the fat on top into a diamond pattern. Place the loin, fat side up, on a rack in a roasting pan. Roast in the center of the oven for 25 minutes.

Meanwhile, melt the butter in a small saucepan. Grate the lemon rind and add it to the pan together with the bread crumbs, parsley, salt and pepper. Mix thoroughly. Take the roasting pan from the oven and increase oven temperature to 400°F. Press the crumb mixture evenly all over the fat side of the meat. Return pan to the oven and roast for 15 to 20 minutes. By that time the crumbs should be crisp and golden brown and the internal temperature of the lamb should be 145°F. If you prefer lamb well done, roast it for 40 minutes before covering it with the crumb mixture.

Part Three
RICE

The word "rice" comes from the Greek *oryza,* which probably goes back to Persian and Sanskrit stems. The western travels of the grain itself parallel those of its name. The armies of Alexander the Great found rice being cultivated in northwest India; eventually it made its way to Persia, and during the spread of Islam was carried to other parts of the Muslim Caliphate. The Moors carried rice and rice cultivation to Spain; from there it reached the marshes of the Po River valley in northern Italy. Like many other foods of Oriental origin, it was taken to England and northern Europe during the Crusades as something of a luxury, and continued to be imported—it could not be profitably grown in those otherwise fertile climates—until the colonization of the New World.

These fragments of history are worth remembering because each new home meant the development of a different local strain of rice with its own flavor and texture. It is estimated that there exist more than 7,000 varieties of rice. Even now the most delicately flavored rices come from its ancient homes, northern India and Persia (Iran). For many centuries the differences among kinds of rice have been taken very seriously there.

"The average Asian can tell blindfold, merely by smelling a dish of cooked rice, what kind of rice it is," writes Charmaine Solomon. "Rice buyers are so trained to recognise the different types of rice that they can hold a few grains in the palm to warm it, sniff it through the hole made by thumb and forefinger, and know its age, its variety, even perhaps where it was grown. Old rice is sought after and prized more than new rice because it tends to cook fluffy and separate, even if the cook absent-mindedly adds too much water. Generally speaking the white polished grains—whether long and fine or small and pearly (much smaller than what we know as short grain rice)—are considered best" (*The Complete Asian Cookbook*).

In India and Persia the long-grain, aromatic, faintly translucent varieties of rice were always held in highest esteem and traditionally reserved for aristocratic dishes. Among the most lavish of these are the *pilau* or *pulao* and *biryani,* all part of a family of elaborate and exquisite rice dishes that are still considered princely. In all of them, rice absorbs fat and liquid while being cooked with other ingredients such as dried fruits, nuts, and cut-up pieces of meat, poultry or fish. Some of the more ceremonial versions are colored with saffron, and the association of rice and saffron has made its way to far distant parts of the world.

There are two main approaches to these aristocratic Persian-Indian rice dishes (well worth trying to cook on their own terms). In one, represented by the Persian *pilau* and the Indian *biryani,* the rice is partly boiled or steamed, then finished with the other ingredients. In the other, typified by Indian *pulao* and most of the many Middle Eastern versions of pilaf, the rice and various aromatic ingredients are first sautéed in butter before the liquid and other ingredients are added. The rice used for such dishes in India and Persia is invariably a long-grain variety that will cook to a delicate but not mushy consistency, with each grain separate. Today the closest equivalent available in this country is Basmati rice from northern India, carried by some Indian markets and specialty stores. It is rare and quite expensive, but exquisite. A fairly good substitute is Texas Patna rice, developed from a strain that originated in the Indian state of Bihar; it is somewhat easier to find than Basmati.

The strains of rice that we associate with Spanish and Italian cooking are less suited to these fluffy-textured dishes. In both regions it was a short-grain rather than long-grain variety that proved best for local growing conditions. Thus, while both areas evolved celebrated rice dishes that clearly stem from the pilafs and pilaus of the Middle East, the final effect is creamier and starchier. Spain developed a family of robust rice dishes redolent of olive oil and vigorously flavored with such ingredients as sautéed onions, garlic, peppers and tomatoes. The rice is the Valencia strain, which clings together much more than the drier Persian and Kashmiri kinds; yet it too is classically gilded with saffron. Often it is simmered in a chicken or seafood broth; the main ingredients are usually chicken, seafood, pork sausages or medleys of all. Traditionally it is cooked in a wide, flat hammered-steel pan called a *paella,* which has given its name to this family of dishes.

The risottos of northern Italy use a still starchier rice, the round-grain Arborio, which can be identified at a glance from the small opaque spot in the center of the stubby white grain. This particular rice is essential to the success of a true risotto. It is possible to make a good paella with American rice, but nothing but Arborio will do for a risotto.

The kinds of rice that spread to the monsoon areas of Asia are still different and require their own kinds of cooking—most often, plain steaming in a small amount of water. In most parts of China, plain rice cooked without seasonings is the daily staple, and it is what is basically meant by the word for food *(fan). Fan* is the precious stuff of necessary nourishment and usually refers to rice, though to a lesser degree noodles and other sustaining cooked cereals may qualify. Other foods—the savory, intricately flavored Chinese meat, poultry, seafood and vegetable preparations that Westerners think of as main dishes—are considered *ts'ai:* garnishes or condiments designed to help one eat the necessary *fan.* Children are taught early never to waste a grain, and to consider the eating of rice as a privilege. In fact, rice is so highly regarded by the Chinese that their equivalent of "How do you do?" quite literally asks, "Have you eaten your rice today?"

The varied genetic possibilities of rice have been more amazingly explored here than in any other region. Both long- and short-grain rices are used in China, and red, yellow, black, fast-maturing, slow-maturing, highland (dry-ground) and lowland (paddy) strains have been known for centuries. For most meals either short- or long-grain rice can be used, depending on regional preferences. For the much-loved breakfast food called *jook* (congee), short-grain rice is always preferred.

Respect for rice is also taught in Japan, where "rice is revered," writes Russ Rudzinski, ". . . the Japanese never losing sight of their dependence on it. The constant reverence is in the word itself, *gohan,* or rice. The Japanese language shows respect or honor to an item by preceding the word with o. For instance, the word for plate is *sara,* but it is often given an honorific o and called *osara.* The word for cooked rice is *han,* but it is always given the highest of honorific prefixes and called *gohan"* *(Japanese Country Cookbook).*

In Japan, the preferred type of rice for all basic cooking is a short-grain starchy variety, similar to the Italian Arborio, that becomes slightly sticky when cooked. In addition, both the Japanese and the Chinese are fond of a particularly sticky variety known as "sweet rice" or "glutinous rice."

American long-grain rice is descended from strains brought by the English to the Carolinas in the seventeenth and eighteenth centuries. Today's Carolina-type grain (now grown mostly in Arkansas, Louisiana, Texas and California) is an excellent all-purpose rice, although it cannot substitute for the translucent, creamy Arborio or the fragrant Basmati rice from India. Wild rice, grown in the northern United States, is considered a great delicacy. It is not, however, a rice at all, but a seed culled from wild grasses.

Throughout Mexico, Central America, the West Indies and most of South America rice is a mainstay of the people and it is often served with beans. These tasty, filling dishes are not only inexpensive but complement each other to form a perfect protein, an adequate substitute for more expensive meat.

If North Americans and northern Europeans have never raised rice cookery to equal the culinary heights of other countries, we have still made some excellent contributions.

Rice pudding can be one of the simplest of desserts—or it can be elevated to the level of the imposing *riz à l'impératrice,* studded with preserved fruits, enriched with *crème anglaise* and whipped cream, and served with puréed berries. Cooked rice takes on a whole new character when bound with a white sauce and deep-fried in croquettes, crisp and nutty on the outside, creamy on the inside.

New Orleans is famed for *calas,* a delicious yeast-raised rice fritter consumed at breakfast with thick, hot coffee. A Creole jambalaya can rival any rice dish in the world, and there are devotees of spicy, hot Cajun red beans and rice who might consider it the best meal ever.

Most recipes that call for rice usually refer to the polished American long-grain variety, but it is worthwhile to seek out special rice when it is called for. Then you can learn to appreciate some of the ways in which the flavor, texture and aroma match the demands of the particular cuisine. When it is cooked with care, this nourishing staple abundantly justifies the honor that has always been lavished on it in the lands of its origin.

RICE

Rice is one of the world's oldest crops and the staple food of millions of its inhabitants. Rich in vitamins and minerals, easily digestible, filling without being fattening at only 31 calories per ounce when cooked, as opposed to more than 70 for bread and potatoes, rice can be used to make hundreds of dishes.

Short-grain and long-grain rice are available everywhere today. Short-grain rice cooks quickly, and becomes moist and tender. Long-grain rice is drier and fluffier when cooked. Two famous types of long-grain rice grown in India are Patna, from the Ganges Plain, and Basmati. Round-grain rice grows in the Po Valley in northern Italy; these grains puff up when cooked.

American rice, primarily long-grain, is grown in Southern states. Brown rice can be short-grain or long-grain and has had only the inedible husk removed. With all the vitamin-B-rich layers still in place, this nutty-flavored rice is the most nutritious. It is also the cheapest to buy and does not take very much longer to cook.

In addition to the natural grains, many kinds of treated or flavored rice are for sale. Converted rice has been processed with steam, and the nu-

Boiling and Baking Rice

1 Place rice in a large saucepan with twice its volume of water. Add ½ to 1 teaspoon salt. Set over moderate heat.

2 Bring water to a boil: stir once to be sure no kernel is sticking to the pan. Cover pan and reduce heat to a simmer.

3 Let long-grain rice cook for 20 minutes. Almost all of the water will be absorbed.

OR To bake rice, put rice and salt in an oven-proof dish and pour in boiling water.

3 Cover the dish and bake at 350°F for 20 minutes, until rice is tender and all water absorbed.

5 Turn cooked rice into a warmed serving dish and fluff with a fork.

trients are preserved. This rice, both white and brown, cooks quickly and never becomes sticky, making it good for casseroles.

Precooked rice is cooked and dried; it needs only to be rehydrated. Boiling water is poured over it; within 10 minutes the water is absorbed and the rice is ready to serve. It is convenient and never becomes sticky, but it is less nutritious than natural rice.

Flavored rices are made of raw or parboiled rice, mixed with spices, de-

hydrated vegetables, sometimes with stock granules. You can make your own flavored rice with homemade stock, herbs and spices.

Rice can be stored for years. In India long-stored rice is considered far superior, and is stored for five years before it is considered digestible. Store it in a cool dry place.

In the United States almost all rice is sold in sealed packages and needs no preliminary washing. If you do buy rice from bales or other loose bundles,

wash it. Measure rice into a fine sieve and lower the sieve into a large bowl of cool water. The rice should stay in the sieve; any foreign matter should float to the surface. Skim off all these bits. If a lot of dust is released in the water, lower the sieve into another bowl of clean water. Let the washed rice drain.

For some recipes rice is soaked before cooking. If your rice has been stored, it may need soaking, just as dried beans do. However, any soaking may cause the loss of some nutrients.

Steaming Rice

4 If you are cooking brown rice, add one quarter more water and simmer for 40 minutes.

1 Place rice and water in a saucepan. Add salt. Bring to a boil and boil for 5 minutes.

2 Drain rice and turn into a steamer. If steamer basket has large holes, line it with cheesecloth.

6 Stir in butter or oil, herbs or cheese. Serve at once, or keep warm over hot water. Do not let rice dry out.

3 Make holes in mound of rice with handle of a wooden spoon. Set steamer basket over already boiling water.

4 Cover steamer and let rice cook for 45 minutes. Do not let water boil away. Add more if needed.

Molding Rice

1 For hot rice molds, coat dishes such as individual cocottes with butter to prevent sticking.

2 Pack hot cooked rice into the buttered molds. Place on a baking sheet and heat at 225°F for 20 minutes.

3 Hot rice may be pressed into large molds such as a soufflé dish or ring mold. A plain mold makes unmolding easier.

4 For cold rice molds, press hot rice into oiled molds and leave until completely cold before turning out.

Boiled rice. The best method for boiling rice is the so-called Oriental method. In this way all nutrients are preserved and the rice swells up to nearly three times its original bulk. Be sure to use a pot of adequate size, generally a 6- to 8-cup saucepan, when

4 portions

8   ounces boned and skinned cooked chicken
2   tablespoons soy sauce
1   tablespoon honey
2   large eggs
1   medium-size onion
4   tablespoons sesame oil
½   cup cooked peas
2   ounces fresh button mushrooms
2   cups cold boiled rice

4 Push vegetables to one side of the pan. Pour in 1 more tablespoon oil, then add beaten eggs.

Buying and Storing Rice

Different types of rice are suitable for different purposes. It is wise to buy with this in mind. Long-grain rice is good to have regularly in stock, as it can be used for a wide range of dishes. Round-grain and short-grain rices are for more specialized tastes and dishes. Buy these in smaller amounts as required.

If possible, buy untreated rice, available at most health-food stores. It is cheaper than converted rice. Also it has more flavor and nutritive value than precooked (dehydrated) rice.

Store rice in a cool dry place and it will keep indefinitely. Jars with tight screwtops are excellent storage containers.

Cooking Rice

Rice can be cooked in any of the following ways:

preparing rice to serve 6. One cup of raw rice makes 6 servings of about ½ cup each. You can use long-grain or round-grain white rice. If you prefer very white, less sticky rice, add 1 teaspoon oil and 2 teaspoons lemon juice to the water. Bring 2 cups water to a boil, add ½ teaspoon salt and 1 cup rice, and return to the boil. Reduce to a simmer, cover tightly, and cook for about 20 minutes, until water is all absorbed and the rice tender. Remove from heat but keep covered for a few minutes longer.

For brown rice use 2½ cups water for each cup of rice and cook for 30 to 40 minutes, until rice is done to your taste.

Baked rice. Use the same proportions of water to rice as for boiled rice. Put rice and salt in a casserole with

Fried Rice with Chicken and Mushrooms

1 Dice chicken and place in a bowl. Mix soy sauce and honey and pour over chicken; stir. Marinate for 2 hours.

2 Beat eggs and set aside. Peel and mince onion. Pour half of oil into a heavy skillet or wok over medium heat.

3 Add onion to oil and stir-fry for 1 minute, until translucent. Add other vegetables and stir-fry for 1 minute.

5 Stir eggs as they cook so they set in threads. Mix egg threads with vegetables. Set aside. Pour remaining oil into a second skillet.

6 Put marinated chicken and any remaining marinade in second pan. Stir-fry for 2 minutes, then remove from heat.

7 Return first pan to medium heat. Add chicken and any oil, then the rice; stir-fry until very hot, about 2 minutes. Serve immediately.

a cover. Bring water to a boil on top of the stove and pour it into the rice. Cover and bake in a preheated 350°F oven for 20 minutes. Brown rice will be done in about 30 to 40 minutes.

Steamed rice. Special rice steamers can be used but the following method will also work successfully.

Boil the rice for 5 minutes as if starting the basic method. Drain off the liquid and put the rice in a steamer basket or the top pan of a vegetable steamer. If the basket holes are large, line the basket with a layer of cheesecloth. Set the basket in place over already boiling water, enough to come just below the basket. Cover the pan and let the rice steam for 45 minutes, or until tender to your taste. Do not let the water in the bottom pan boil away; add more boiling water if needed.

Cooked rice can be kept hot for up to 30 minutes. Cover the pan and set it over hot water in a low oven, 225°F.

If you plan to use the rice cold, spread it out on a large platter to let steam escape quickly. When it is cold, cover and refrigerate. If the rice is to be used for salad, you may stir in some of the dressing while the rice is still hot; it will absorb more of the dressing and become more flavorful.

Wild rice. This can be cooked like any other, using 2½ to 3 cups water to 1 cup grains, and allowing 1 hour over *very* low heat. However, there is a better method, which produces an even more delicious rice, swelled to its maximum bulk. Cover 1 cup wild rice with 4 cups cold water and let it soak overnight. Next day use a sieve to lift out the grains to a clean 8-cup saucepan. Discard the soaking water, which may be full of dust particles. Bring 4 cups fresh water to a boil and pour it over the grains. Let it stand until the water is cool. Set the pan over heat and bring it slowly to a boil. Sprinkle in ½ teaspoon salt. Reduce heat to a bare simmer and let the rice cook for 30 to 40 minutes, until all the little hulls have opened and the kernels have swelled to about four times the original size. The water may not be all absorbed; use any that remains to add

Risotto Milanese

6 portions

1	medium-size mild onion
1	ounce beef marrow
6	tablespoons unsalted butter
1½	cups round-grain (Arborio) rice
½	cup dry white wine
5	cups chicken stock
¾	teaspoon whole saffron
¼	cup grated Parmesan cheese

1 Peel and mince onion. Scoop marrow out of beef bones. Chop and weigh marrow.

4 Add the marrow and cook until melted, about 3 minutes.

5 Add rice. Stir to coat all kernels with butter and marrow, but cook only until grains are opaque.

8 Continue adding the hot stock ⅓ cup at a time, but set ½ cup aside for the saffron infusion.

9 Soak saffron in reserved stock for 10 to 15 minutes. Strain. Use as last addition of stock.

2 Melt 4 tablespoons of the butter in a heavy pan over moderate heat.

3 When butter has stopped foaming, add onion and cook for about 4 minutes.

6 Pour in wine. Cook, stirring, until wine is all absorbed. Meanwhile, set stock over low heat.

7 Add ⅓ cup hot stock to rice and cook, stirring, until stock has been absorbed.

10 When all stock has been added and absorbed, test a grain of rice. It should be soft and creamy.

11 Stir grated cheese and remaining butter into hot rice. When cheese has melted, serve risotto without delay.

to stock or soup as it will be full of nutrients.

Flavored Rice. Rice can be flavored in many ways, and can be combined with countless ingredients. One of the easiest ways to add flavor is to cook rice in homemade chicken or beef stock instead of water. Sautéed onions, mushrooms or crumbled cooked bacon can be added to the stock-cooked rice. Minced fresh herbs (chives, parsley, thyme, fennel, to name a few) are well suited to buttered rice, and a sprinkling of nuts and raisins adds the perfect touch to curry-flavored rice.

Molded Rice. Rice can be molded, hot or cold. For hot rice, press it firmly into well-*buttered* molds—individual cocottes, large molds or ring molds. Set the molds on a baking sheet and heat in a 225°F oven for 20 minutes. For cold rice molds, pack hot rice into *oiled* molds and leave until absolutely cold before turning them out.

Fried Rice. This favorite Chinese dish should be attractive and fresh looking; true fried rice is not a ragtag mixture of leftovers. Cook the rice at least one day ahead and let it become completely cold. Use oil only (no butter); it may be peanut, corn or sesame oil, and it should be used sparingly.

Risotto. This is an Italian rice dish that always includes additional ingredients; it is not just plain boiled rice. It is creamy, and like Italian pasta should be *al dente,* but each grain is separate with distinctive flavor and texture. For best results use Italian (Arborio) round-grain rice. Butter is almost always used in risotto, but it is possible to use oil. Risotto alla Milanese traditionally includes beef marrow, about 1 tablespoon per serving. If you do not have it, add a little more butter. Both wine and stock are used. The wine may be white wine, dry Marsala, even Champagne. Vegetables, meat, poultry, shellfish and cheese can all be added to make different risotto mixtures. Shellfish are added raw since they cook so quickly; meat and poultry should be cooked before starting the risotto. Cheese is stirred in at the end. In Italy risotto is served as a separate course, like pasta.

Pilau, Pilaf, Pulao, Polo. The Indian rice dishes, *pilau* and *pulao,* are "dry curries" since they are flavored with curry spices and are dry, without sauce, when finished. *Pilaf* is Middle Eastern, *pulao* South Indian. *Polo,* which is Persian, is prepared without the curry spices. Use natural long-grain raw rice for all of them.

The fat used in this cookery is usually oil for pilaf, clarified butter or *ghee* for pulao and polo. Water is used for soaking rice for pilau. For all the dishes, remaining liquid may be water or stock. Spices—always whole for pulao—include cardamom, cumin-seed, cinnamon, cloves, turmeric. Onion is essential. Raisins and other fruits and chopped nuts may be used.

The most important piece of equipment needed to make any of these dishes is a heavy-based pan or casserole dish. A heavy base is essential as very slow cooking is required to make the rice absorb the liquid and become tender and full of flavor. To finish the dishes, you will need a thick, clean cloth to put over the rice. This helps the rice to steam and become tender.

Pilau. Soak the rice in twice its weight of water. Prepare the spices by grinding them in a spice mill or pounding in a mortar. Prepare the onion. Heat the butter until hot but not brown; add the onion and cook until soft. Add spices and stir to mix onion and spices together. Drain the soaked rice, add to the pan, and stir until all the kernels are coated with butter. Add the cold liquid, bring to a boil, then reduce heat and simmer for 10 minutes, until all water has been absorbed and the top of the rice is pitted with holes. Reduce heat to very low, cover rice with a folded cloth, then with the cover of the pan. Let the mixture steam for 25 minutes.

Pulao is made in the same fashion, but the rice is not soaked first, and the spices are always used whole and served with the rice. The finished pulao is garnished with raisins, nuts, onion rings and whatever the recipe calls for.

Pilaf can be made like a risotto. Use brown rice or any long-grain white rice. Add liquid all at once. If meat is used in the pilaf, it should be cut into bite-size pieces. Brown the meat on all sides, then cook in liquid until the pieces are tender and remaining liquid is well flavored with meat juices. Add the rice, cover the pan, and simmer the mixture undisturbed for 20 to 30 minutes, until rice is tender and the liquid all absorbed. The dish is served with chutney.

Chelo is plain rice cooked Persian style. Rinse rice, then soak overnight. The next day drain the rice, cook it in salted water for 15 minutes, then drain again. Pour melted butter into a deep heavy pan and spoon rice into the pan, layer by layer, shaping a cone. Pour melted butter on top. Cover the pan with a cloth and lid, so no steam escapes, then cook over low heat until the cone of rice is white and tender while the bottom forms a crisp golden crust.

Polo is piled up in the same way, but a thick meat or vegetable stew is layered in the rice.

Spanish Rice, Mexican Dry Rice Soup. Finally, here are rice dishes from the Americas. Spanish rice is cooked in the American Southwest and in Mexico. Dry rice soup is not a soup, but a dish like a risotto, served as a separate course after the "wet soup." It is true that rice was introduced by the Spaniards, but it has now been part of Mexican cuisine for more than 300 years.

For dry rice soup, soak the rice in hot water for 15 minutes, then drain, rinse and drain again. Use 2 tablespoons oil for 1 cup rice. Heat the oil and sauté the rice in it until golden. Pour in 3 cups puréed vegetables mixed with stock and add seasoning to taste. Bring to a boil, reduce to a simmer, and cook for 20 to 30 minutes, until rice is tender and most of the liquid is absorbed. The mixture should be moist, not dry. The vegetables used include tomatoes, chili peppers, onions and garlic. Sometimes a vegetable dye such as annatto seed is used to color the rice. Tomatoes produce pink rice, green chilies green rice.

Pilau

4 portions

¾	cup Basmati or other long-grain rice
4	cardamom pods
2	teaspoons whole cuminseeds
1	small onion
2	tablespoons clarified butter
1	teaspoon ground turmeric
1	bay leaf
	pinch of salt
½	cup golden raisins

4 Add onion to butter and cook for about 3 minutes, stirring from time to time.

8 Reduce heat and simmer uncovered 10 minutes, until almost all liquid has been absorbed.

1 Put rice in a bowl and pour in 1 cup cold water. Soak rice for at least 4 hours.

2 Remove cardamom seeds from pods and drop into a mortar with cuminseeds. Crush spices with a pestle.

3 Peel and mince the onion. Melt the butter in a heavy pan over low heat.

5 Stir in crushed spices and ground turmeric. Stir well to coat onion with the spice mixture.

6 Drain rice and add it to the pan. Stir briskly to coat the grains with butter and spice mixture.

7 Pour in 1 generous cup of cold water and add bay leaf, salt and raisins. Bring water to a boil.

9 Fold a clean towel into four and place it over the pan of rice. Cover pan tightly with the lid.

10 Leave pan undisturbed over very low heat. After 25 minutes, remove cover and fluff the rice.

11 Turn cooked rice into a warmed serving dish. Serve immediately with curry or a stew.

Lamb and Apricot Polo

6 portions

- This is an economical dish as it makes a small amount of lamb go a long way. It also uses a relatively inexpensive cut of lamb.

- Dried apricots are always used in this recipe. There is no need to soak them first as they absorb liquid during cooking.

1	cup long-grain (preferably Basmati) rice
1	teaspoon salt
1	medium-size onion
4	ounces butter
12	ounces boned lamb shoulder, cubed
¼	cup seedless raisins
½	cup dried apricots
½	teaspoon ground cinnamon

1 Boil the rice in 2 cups salted water for 8 minutes. Drain, rinse with cold water, leave until cold.

5 Cover with warm water and simmer, covered, for 1½ hours, until meat is tender.

9 Place folded towel over the rice to cover, then cover casserole with the lid.

2 Peel and mince onion. Melt 4 tablespoons of the butter. Add onion and sauté until soft.

3 Add lamb cubes, turning pieces so all sides are coated with butter.

4 Add fruits, turning pieces so all sides of fruits are buttered. Add cinnamon.

6 Use remaining butter to coat a heavy casserole or flameproof dish with a lid.

7 Make a layer of rice ½ inch thick in base of dish. Cover with a layer of meat and fruits.

8 Continue layering, finishing with rice. Fold a clean dish towel into four.

10 Place over very low heat and steam for 20 minutes, until rice is tender and has absorbed sauce.

11 When cooking time is up, remove lid and cloth. If you wish, serve polo from the casserole.

OR Turn polo into a warmed serving dish and mix rice and meat together before serving.

Yunnan Quick-Fried Shrimps on Crackling Rice

4 portions

1	medium-size onion
8	ounces raw shrimps
8	ounces boneless chicken breast
2	tablespoons sesame oil
7	teaspoons cornstarch
¾	cup beef stock
2	tablespoons tomato purée
1½	tablespoons soy sauce
1½	tablespoons sugar

1½	tablespoons wine vinegar
2	tablespoons dry sherry
6	cups cooked long-grain rice
5	to 6 cups vegetable oil for deep-frying
1	teaspoon salt
1	teaspoon freshly ground white pepper

Peel and mince the onion. Shell and devein the shrimps. Cut chicken breast meat into 1-inch cubes. Preheat oven to 275°F. Heat sesame oil in a large skillet; add minced onion and sauté until softened. Blend 4 teaspoons of the cornstarch into the beef stock. Add to the skillet, stirring, and stir in tomato purée, soy sauce, sugar, vinegar and sherry. Simmer sauce for 1 minute, stirring. Remove from heat and reserve.

Spread the cooked rice in a shallow baking pan; place in the oven to dry the rice slightly.

Fill a deep-fryer or a wok one third full of vegetable oil and heat the oil to 360°F. Sprinkle shrimps and chicken with salt, white pepper and remaining 3 teaspoons cornstarch; rub in the mixture with fingers. Place shrimps and chicken cubes in a frying basket, immerse in the hot oil, and fry for 1 minute. Drain on paper towels. Stir drained shrimps and chicken into the sauce reserved in the skillet; heat until just hot.

Remove rice from the oven and place in a fine-meshed frying basket. Immerse rice in the hot oil and fry for 1½ minutes. Remove rice from basket and drain on paper towels. Place rice on a warmed serving platter. Spoon the sauce with the shrimps and chicken on top and serve at once.

Risi e Bisi

(Venetian Rice with Peas)

4 portions

1	small onion	6	cups chicken stock, hot
6	tablespoons unsalted butter	1	cup round-grain (Arborio) rice
⅓	cup diced cooked ham or prosciutto	1	ounce Parmesan cheese, grated (¼ cup)
1½	cups shelled fresh green peas		

Peel and mince the onion. Melt 4 tablespoons of the butter in a large saucepan over moderate heat. Add ham, onion and peas; cook for 1 minute, stirring frequently. Pour in ½ cup hot stock and bring to a boil. Add the rice, then 2 cups hot stock. Cover and cook for 20 minutes, until liquid is absorbed. Add remaining hot stock in 2 additions. When all the stock has been absorbed and rice is creamy and soft, stir in remaining 2 tablespoons butter and the grated cheese.

Risi e bisi is more moist than a standard risotto, but the rice kernels are still separate and not sticky.

Rice with Four Cheeses

4 portions

1 cup round-grain (Arborio) rice	½ cup cubed bel paese cheese
2 cups water	½ cup cubed Gruyère cheese
¾ teaspoon salt	4 tablespoons unsalted butter
¾ cup cubed ham or tongue	2 ounces Parmesan cheese, grated (½ cup)
½ cup cubed provolone cheese	

Place rice, water and salt in a large saucepan and cook rice until tender; the water should be absorbed. Mix cubed meat and cheeses in a bowl. Preheat oven to 400°F. Butter a 6-cup baking dish.

Layer one third of the rice in the buttered dish and sprinkle with half of the meat and cheeses. Cut butter into small bits and sprinkle one third of the bits over the cheese layer. Repeat with another third of the rice and remaining meat and cheeses, dot with another third of the butter, and finish with remaining rice. Dot the top with the last of the butter and sprinkle with the Parmesan cheese. Set the baking dish in a large pan and add water to reach halfway up the sides of the baking dish. Bake the casserole for 30 minutes, until top is golden. Serve from the baking dish.

Indian Rice with Eggplant and Potatoes

6 portions

1½	cups long-grain rice
12	ounces potatoes
1	large eggplant, 1 to 1¼ pounds
1½	teaspoons salt
1	teaspoon ground turmeric
1	teaspoon ground cuminseed

1	tablespoon ground coriander
½	teaspoon cayenne pepper
½	teaspoon sugar
1	tablespoon lemon juice
2	teaspoons chick-pea flour
½	cup melted clarified butter

Soak the rice in cold water for 30 minutes; drain. While the rice is soaking, peel the potatoes and cut into ½-inch cubes; cover them with water to prevent discoloration. Peel the eggplant, cut into cubes, and soak in salt water for 30 minutes.

Put drained rice in a large saucepan, pour in 3 cups water, and add 1 teaspoon of the salt. Bring to a boil, cover, reduce heat to very low, and simmer for 15 to 20 minutes, until the rice is tender and all the water has been absorbed. Remove pan from heat, but keep the rice warm.

In a small mixing bowl combine all the spices, the sugar, lemon juice, chick-pea flour and remaining ½ teaspoon salt. Mix to a paste, adding more lemon juice if necessary. Preheat oven to 350°F.

Heat ¼ cup of the clarified butter in a large frying pan over moderate heat. Drain potatoes and eggplant and pat dry on paper towels. Add them to the butter and sauté, stirring frequently, for 5 minutes. Add the spice paste and continue to sauté, stirring, for 10 minutes; add a spoonful or two of water if the mixture becomes too dry. Cover the pan, reduce heat to low, and cook the vegetables for 10 to 15 minutes, until tender.

Spread half of the hot rice over the bottom of a 2-quart baking dish. Sprinkle 2 tablespoons melted butter over the rice. Spread the vegetable mixture and all the butter and spices from the pan over the rice. Cover with remaining rice and sprinkle remaining melted butter on top. Cover the dish and place in the oven. Bake for 20 to 25 minutes, until ingredients are very hot. Serve from the baking dish.

Nasi Goreng

(Indonesian Fried Rice)

4 portions

2	medium-size onions	¾	cup diced cooked chicken
1	garlic clove	2	tablespoons soy sauce
4	ounces raw shrimps	1½	tablespoons lemon juice
4	tablespoons peanut oil	1	teaspoon brown sugar
3	large eggs	4	cups cooked long-grain
2	firm tomatoes		rice
1	teaspoon chili powder		

Peel and mince onions and garlic. Shell and devein the shrimps. Heat 1 tablespoon of the oil in a large skillet over moderate heat. Beat the eggs lightly and pour into the skillet. Cook without stirring until the bottom of the eggs is set, about 2 minutes. Turn and cook just until the second side is set. Transfer eggs to a warmed plate and cover loosely with foil. Wash tomatoes and cut into ¼-inch slices.

Heat remaining oil in the same skillet. Add onions,

garlic and chili powder and stir-fry for 1 minute. Add shrimps, diced chicken, soy sauce, lemon juice and brown sugar; stir-fry for 2 to 3 minutes. Add rice and stir-fry for 2 minutes more, until rice is heated through.

Turn rice onto a warmed platter. Cut omelet into strips and arrange them in a lattice over the rice. Decorate edges of the dish with tomato slices.

Risotto with Chicken and Vegetables

6 portions

6	slices of smoked bacon	½	teaspoon dried thyme
1	pound boned chicken breast	1	teaspoon salt
2	medium-size onions	½	teaspoon black pepper
2	large green peppers	¼	teaspoon celery salt
8	ounces fresh button mushrooms	¼	teaspoon cayenne pepper
5	medium-size tomatoes	2	teaspoons Worcestershire sauce (optional)
4	tablespoons butter	2	cups chicken stock
1½	cups long-grain rice	2	ounces Parmesan cheese, grated (½ cup)
1¼	cups canned whole corn kernels		

Cut bacon slices into small dice. Remove any skin from the chicken and cut the meat into thin strips. Peel onions, cut into moderately thick slices, and separate slices into rings. Wash peppers, halve them, discard stems, seeds and ribs, and chop peppers. Wipe mushrooms with a damp cloth; trim base of stems and cut caps and stems into quarters. Blanch and peel the tomatoes; chop them, discarding as many seeds as possible.

Put the bacon dice in a medium-size flameproof casserole and fry bacon over moderate heat for 5 minutes, until it is crisp and golden and has rendered most of its fat. Turn bacon to cook all pieces evenly. Transfer to paper towels to

drain, then put on a plate and set aside. Pour off the bacon fat.

Melt 2 tablespoons of the butter in the casserole. Add chicken strips and sauté them, stirring frequently, for about 6 minutes, until strips are lightly browned on all sides. Transfer chicken to the plate with the bacon. Put onions and peppers in the casserole and sauté, stirring frequently, for 5 minutes. Add the mushrooms and cook, stirring, for 3 minutes longer. Use a slotted spoon to remove vegetables from the casserole; add them to the chicken and bacon.

Melt remaining butter in the casserole. Add the rice and stir over moderate heat for 3 minutes. Stir in the chicken, bacon, sautéed vegetables, tomatoes, corn, thyme, salt, black pepper, celery salt, cayenne, and Worcestershire if you are using it. Mix everything well. Pour in the stock and bring to a boil. Stir once to mix everything. Reduce heat to low, cover the casserole, and simmer for 20 to 25 minutes, until rice is tender and has absorbed all the liquid.

Pile the risotto on a warmed serving platter, sprinkle the Parmesan cheese on top, and serve immediately.

Risotto with Shrimps

4 to 6 portions

1	medium-size onion	2	cups round-grain (Arborio) rice
1	garlic clove	½	cup dry white wine
1	pound small shrimps	5	cups chicken stock, boiling
½	teaspoon whole saffron	2	ounces Parmesan cheese, grated (½ cup)
4	ounces butter		

Peel onion and cut into thin slices. Peel garlic and put through a press into the onion. Shell and devein the shrimps. Crush the saffron and soak it in 1 tablespoon hot water. Melt 6 tablespoons of the butter in a large saucepan over moderate heat. Add onion and garlic and cook, stirring occasionally, for 5 to 7 minutes, until onion is soft and translucent. Add rice to the pan and cook for 5 minutes, stirring with a wooden spatula to coat all the kernels with butter. Pour in the wine and about one third of the boiling stock. Adjust heat so liquid is bubbling gently. When the liquid is absorbed, pour in another third of the stock. Continue with the last of the stock; when that batch is absorbed, the rice should be tender and moist but still firm.

Stir in the shrimps and cook for 2 minutes. Stir in the saffron infusion, remaining butter and the grated cheese. Leave over heat for 1 minute, gently stirring to mix ingredients. Transfer risotto to a warmed serving dish.

Carrot Polo

4 portions

1 cup short-grain rice	4 tablespoons butter
salt	1 tablespoon sugar
1 pound carrots	½ teaspoon ground cinnamon
1 large onion	

Put the rice in a saucepan with ½ teaspoon salt and pour in 2 cups water. Bring to a boil, reduce heat to keep water bubbling gently, and cook for 8 minutes. Drain rice and spread out on a platter to let the steam escape. Scrub and scrape the carrots, then grate them by hand or in a food processor fitted with the shredding disc. Peel and mince the onion. Melt 3 tablespoons of the butter in a heavy pan over low heat. Add the onion and sauté until soft. Add grated carrots, sugar and cinnamon and sauté gently for 10 minutes, stirring frequently. Taste, and add salt or more sugar if necessary.

Coat a heavy flameproof casserole with remaining butter. Make alternate layers of rice and carrot mixture, ending with rice. Cover the casserole with a cloth, then with the lid. Steam over low heat for 30 minutes. Serve from the casserole, spooning out some of the crisp golden layer on the bottom.

Variation: For rice with dates and almonds, sauté 4 ounces of split blanched almonds in 4 ounces butter until golden. Add ¼ cup raisins and ½ cup chopped pitted dates and sauté gently for 3 minutes. Add ½ cup water, cover, and simmer for 15 minutes, until liquid has been absorbed. Layer the almond and fruit mixture with the partly cooked rice, dot top with butter, and steam for 30 minutes in the same fashion as for carrot polo.

Jambalaya

(Rice and Shrimps, Creole Style)

4 portions

3	slices of lean bacon	½	teaspoon cayenne pepper
1	medium-size onion	1	bay leaf
2	celery ribs	2	cups canned peeled tomatoes, undrained
1	large green pepper		
1	tablespoon vegetable oil	¾	cup chopped cooked ham
1½	cups long-grain rice	1	pound shelled raw shrimps, deveined
3	cups chicken stock		
½	teaspoon salt	½	cup chopped cooked chicken
½	teaspoon freshly ground pepper	1	tablespoon chopped fresh parsley

Chop bacon. Peel and mince onion; wash, dry, and chop celery. Wash green pepper, halve it, discard stem, seeds and ribs, and chop pepper. Heat the oil in a large saucepan. Add bacon and fry until crisp and brown. Remove bacon pieces with a slotted spoon and drain on paper towels. Pour off excess fat from the saucepan, leaving about 2 tablespoons. Add the onion to the pan and sauté until golden brown. Stir in the celery, then the rice. Cook, stirring constantly with a wooden spoon, until rice is coated with fat. Pour in the stock and add salt, black pepper, cayenne and bay leaf; simmer, covered, for 10 minutes.

Add chopped green pepper and the tomatoes with their liquid to the pan; simmer, covered, for 5 minutes. Add the ham, shrimps, chicken and bacon pieces; stir well. Cover and cook over low heat until the rice is tender and all ingredients heated through, about 10 minutes longer. Transfer jambalaya to a warmed serving dish and sprinkle with parsley.

Pork Pilaf

4 portions

1 cup long-grain rice	3 slices of bacon
salt	1 cup canned tomatoes
8 ounces onions	freshly ground black
1 garlic clove	pepper
4 ounces fresh mushrooms	1 teaspoon sugar
3 tablespoons oil	1 bay leaf
1 pound pork chops (about 2)	1 teaspoon dried thyme
	4 ounces frozen peas

Pour the rice into a large pan; add 2 cups water and 1 teaspoon salt. Set the pan over moderate heat, stir once, and bring to a boil. Reduce heat, cover the pan, and simmer for 8 minutes. Drain the rice, rinse with cold water, drain again, and fluff with a fork. Spread out on a large plate to cool.

Peel and mince the onions. Peel the garlic and put through a press into the onions. Wipe mushrooms with a damp cloth, trim base of stems, and slice caps and stems. Heat the oil in a large skillet or flameproof casserole. Add onions and garlic and sauté for 3 minutes. Cut off all bones and gristle from the pork and cut the meat into bite-size pieces. Add the meat to the pan of onions. Chop the bacon and add to the pan of onions, along with the sliced mushrooms. Add canned tomatoes and mash them to a pulp with a fork. Add ½ teaspoon salt, pepper to taste, the sugar and herbs and cook for 10 minutes. Stir in the peas.

Add the cooled rice and 1 cup water to the skillet or casserole. Bring the pilaf back to a boil, reduce heat, and simmer, covered, for 20 minutes, until rice has absorbed all the liquid. If you have cooked the pilaf in a casserole, serve it from the casserole. If you have cooked it in a skillet, transfer it to a warmed serving bowl.

Turkish Chicken Pilaf

6 portions

1 cup long-grain rice	½ teaspoon ground cinnamon
salt	2 tablespoons tomato purée
1 pound boned chicken breast	2 ripe tomatoes, about 1 pound total
1 large onion	1 small red bell pepper
3 tablespoons olive oil	3 tablespoons chopped fresh parsley
black pepper	

Put rice in a saucepan with ½ teaspoon salt and pour in 2 cups water. Bring to a boil and cook for 8 minutes. Drain rice and spread out on a plate to release steam.

Remove skin and any cartilage from chicken and cut into ¾-inch cubes. Peel and chop the onion. Heat the oil in a deep skillet over moderate heat. Add onion and sauté until translucent. Add chicken and sauté for 4 minutes, turning so all sides are sealed. Season with salt and pepper and stir in the cinnamon. Mix the tomato purée with 3 tablespoons water and stir into the skillet. Reduce heat so the mixture is just simmering.

Blanch and peel the tomatoes. Chop them, and remove as many seeds as possible. Wash and halve the pepper, discard stem, seeds and ribs, and cut pepper into small pieces. Add vegetables to the skillet and sprinkle with parsley. Add enough water to cover the vegetables and bring to a boil. Reduce heat and simmer, covered, for 45 minutes. The meat will be tender and the sauce thick. Stir in the rice with another cup of water. Bring to a boil, reduce heat, cover, and simmer for 30 minutes, until rice is tender and has absorbed most of the liquid.

Variation: This pilaf can be made with lamb, which is actually more typical in Turkey. Use 1 pound boned lamb from leg or shoulder, cut into cubes, and simmer the mixture in the skillet for 1 hour, until lamb is tender.

Risotto with Zucchini

4 to 6 portions

2	garlic cloves		¾	cup dry white wine
1	pound small zucchini		2	cups round-grain (Arborio) rice
4	ounces butter		4	cups chicken stock, boiling
1	teaspoon salt		2	ounces Parmesan cheese, grated (½ cup)
1	teaspoon black pepper			
1¾	cups canned peeled tomatoes			

Peel garlic cloves. Wash and trim zucchini and cut them into ½-inch cubes. Melt 6 tablespoons of the butter in a large saucepan over moderate heat. Put the garlic cloves through a press into the butter and cook for 1 minute. Add zucchini cubes and cook, stirring and turning occasionally, for about 6 minutes, until they are lightly browned but still somewhat crisp. Stir in the salt, pepper, tomatoes with the can juice, and the wine. Bring to a boil, stirring. Add the rice, reduce heat to low, stir once, and cook for 5 minutes. Pour in one third of the boiling stock. Adjust heat so the liquid is bubbling evenly.

When the liquid is absorbed, add another third of the stock. When that amount is absorbed, pour in the rest and cook until rice is tender and moist but still firm. Remove pan from heat.

Stir in remaining butter and the grated cheese; mix gently to blend but do not stir more than that. Cover for 1 minute to let the cheese melt in retained heat of the mixture. Transfer to a warmed serving bowl and serve as a luncheon or supper main dish or as an accompaniment to chicken or fish.

Mexican Dry Rice Soup

6 portions

1¾	cups long-grain rice		4	tablespoons olive oil
1	medium-size Spanish onion		1	cup cooked green peas
3	garlic cloves		4	fresh red chili peppers
2	cups canned tomatoes		1	large avocado
½	teaspoon paprika			lemon juice
3	cups chicken stock			sprigs of fresh coriander

Soak the rice in hot water for 15 minutes; drain, rinse, and drain again. Peel and mince the onion. Peel garlic cloves and put through a press into the onion. Place onion, garlic and canned tomatoes in a blender container or in the bowl of a food processor and whirl for about 5 seconds. (If you lack either appliance, put the tomatoes through a food mill and leave the onion and garlic chopped.) Stir paprika into the mixture. Pour the stock into a saucepan and set over moderate heat.

Heat the oil in a heavy saucepan over moderate heat. Reduce heat and add the rice. Stir with a wooden spatula for about 3 minutes, until rice is well coated with oil. Add tomato mixture and hot stock; stir. Reduce heat to very low and cover the saucepan. Cook for about 25 minutes, until rice has absorbed the liquid. Fold the cooked peas into the rice and leave over heat until peas are warmed. Remove the saucepan from heat.

Meanwhile, wearing rubber or plastic gloves, slice the chili peppers from tip to stem end, making about 5 slices attached at the stem end, so that the slices will open out like a flower. Remove seeds and ribs. Peel, pit and slice the avocado. Dip slices into lemon juice to prevent browning.

Spoon the rice into a warmed serving bowl. Garnish with the chili flowers, avocado slices and coriander sprigs.

Brown Rice Salad with Walnuts

4 portions

2 cups cooked brown rice, cooled
½ cup chopped walnuts
½ cup seedless raisins
¾ cup sliced celery
¼ cup chopped flat-leaf parsley

¾ cup olive oil
  juice of 1 lemon
1 teaspoon Worcestershire sauce
  salt and black pepper
1 garlic clove
8 crisp romaine leaves

Combine rice, walnuts, raisins, celery and parsley in a large mixing bowl. In another bowl, combine oil, lemon juice, Worcestershire sauce and salt and pepper to taste. Peel garlic and put through a press into the dressing. Beat dressing until well combined. Pour it over the salad ingredients and toss lightly to mix. At this point the salad may be covered and chilled.

Before serving, let the salad reach room temperature, as it is more flavorful when not ice cold. Line a salad bowl with the romaine leaves and mound the rice salad in the center.

Yellow Rice

4 to 6 portions

4 tablespoons butter
1½ cups long-grain rice
1 teaspoon ground turmeric
1 teaspoon salt

½ cup seedless golden raisins
1 cinnamon stick
1 bay leaf
3 cups boiling water

Melt the butter in a saucepan over moderate heat. Add the rice, reduce heat to moderately low, and sauté the rice for 5 minutes, stirring with a wooden spatula to coat all the grains with butter. Add turmeric, salt, raisins, cinnamon and bay leaf, and stir well to mix. Pour in the boiling water and increase heat to high until water returns to the boil. Reduce heat to low, cover the pan, and cook rice for 15 minutes, until it is tender and all the water has been absorbed. Discard bay leaf and cinnamon stick. Turn rice into a warmed serving dish.

Lemon Rice

4 portions

1½ cups long-grain rice
3 cups water
1 teaspoon salt
4 eggs
6 ounces Parmesan cheese, grated (1½ cups)

  grated rind of 2 lemons
2 tablespoons fresh lemon juice
2 tablespoons butter

Place the rice in a large saucepan; pour in the water and add the salt. Bring water to a boil over high heat, cover the pan, reduce heat to low, and simmer for 15 to 20 minutes, until rice is tender and all liquid has been absorbed. If liquid is absorbed before rice is tender, add more boiling water, ¼ cup at a time. Remove pan from heat.

In a mixing bowl beat the eggs, cheese, lemon rind and juice together with a fork until well blended. Melt the butter in a 2-quart flameproof casserole over moderate heat. Spoon rice into the casserole and reduce heat to low. Pour in the egg mixture, stirring gently all the while, until rice and eggs are mixed before any part of the egg mixture cooks into a scrambled egg texture. Cook for 4 to 5 minutes, until the cheese is melted. Remove casserole from heat and spoon the lemon rice onto a warmed serving dish. Serve without delay.

Wild Rice with Mushrooms

6 portions

1 large onion	3 cups chicken stock
1 celery rib	1 teaspoon salt
8 ounces fresh button mushrooms	½ teaspoon freshly ground pepper
1⅓ cups wild rice	½ cup toasted slivered almonds
4 tablespoons unsalted butter	

Peel and mince onion; wash, dry and chop celery. Wipe mushrooms with a damp cloth; trim base of stems and cut caps and stems into halves. Rinse and drain the rice. Melt the butter in a large saucepan over moderate heat. Add onion and celery and stir-fry for 5 to 7 minutes, until onion is translucent. Add rice and mushrooms; sauté for 3 minutes, stirring all the time. Pour in 2 cups of the stock and add salt and pepper. Bring to a boil, reduce heat, cover, and simmer for 45 minutes, until rice has puffed and liquid has been absorbed. Check after 15 minutes and add more of the stock if needed; check again after 30 minutes.

Spoon the mixture onto a warmed serving dish. Sprinkle with almonds and serve at once.

Persian Tomato Pilaf

6 portions

1½ cups long-grain rice	freshly ground black pepper
salt	1 teaspoon sugar
2 pounds fresh plum tomatoes	1 bay leaf
8 ounces onions	3 tablespoons minced fresh parsley or mixed parsley and mint
3 tablespoons olive oil	

Put rice and 1 teaspoon salt in a large saucepan and pour in 3 cups water. Bring to a boil and boil for 8 minutes. Drain rice and spread out on a platter to release steam. Blanch and peel tomatoes, chop them, and discard as many seeds as possible. Peel and mince the onions. Heat the oil in a large heavy saucepan and sauté onions for 3 minutes. Add chopped tomatoes and season with ½ teaspoon salt and pepper to taste. Stir in the sugar. Cook for 4 minutes, then mash tomatoes with a fork. Add bay leaf and simmer for 10 minutes. Add the partly cooked rice and 1 cup water. Bring to a boil, reduce heat, cover, and simmer for 20 minutes. Sprinkle with fresh herbs.

Variation: For eggplant pilaf to serve cold, cut 1 pound eggplant into chunks. Sauté in olive oil, turning often, until browned all over. Mix the eggplant with the partly cooked rice, dot with butter, and steam for 30 minutes. Serve cold with plain yogurt.

Spanish Rice

4 portions

2	onions	3	tablespoons olive oil
1	garlic clove	½	cup pitted green olives
1	green bell pepper	1	teaspoon dried orégano
2	red bell peppers	½	teaspoon dried basil
12	ounces fresh mushrooms	½	teaspoon salt
1¾	cups canned peeled tomatoes	¼	teaspoon black pepper
		2	cups cooked rice

Peel and slice the onions. Peel garlic and put through a press into the onions. Wash green and red peppers, halve them, discard stems, seeds and ribs, and cut peppers from top to bottom into thin slices. Wipe mushrooms with a damp cloth, trim base of stems, and slice caps and stems. Chop the tomatoes, reserving the can juice. Heat the oil in a large frying pan over moderate heat. Add onions and garlic and cook, stirring constantly, for 5 to 7 minutes, until onions are soft and translucent. Add green and red peppers and cook for 4 minutes, stirring frequently. Add mushrooms, tomatoes with the can juice, olives, orégano, basil, salt and pepper, and cook for 3 minutes.

Add the rice to the vegetables and cook for 3 to 4 minutes, until the rice is heated through. Stir to mix rice with the other ingredients, but do not stir constantly because that tends to break up the rice kernels. Transfer the mixture to a warmed serving platter. Serve with broiled meat or fish.

Part Four

FRUIT DESSERTS

LITTLE APPLES

When God had made the oak trees
    And the beeches and the pines,
    And the flowers and the grasses,
    And the tendrils and the vines,
He saw that there was wanting
A something in His plan,
    And He made the little apples,
    The little cider apples;
    The sharp, sour, cider apples,
To prove His love for man.
                    Anonymous

The very first dessert was surely fruit—a crisp red apple fallen from a tree, or else a very sweet and juicy fig, a luscious peach, a fragrant apricot . . . a gift from nature to satisfy our yen for sweets. From the first bite Eve took of the forbidden apple, fruit played an important role in history, mythology, religion, folklore, magic, medicine and cuisine.

The apple seems to play a leading role, perhaps because symbolically and even linguistically it represents all fruits. Most probably the famous golden apples that brought about the Trojan War were really oranges or lemons.

The pregnant Virgin Mary, it is told and sung, longed for a taste of some ripe fruit she saw way up on a high branch. Joseph was uncooperative, so the tree obliged by bending down its branches, allowing Mary to pick the apples for herself, only some versions say it was a cherry tree.

Apricots grown in the Hunza valley in Tibet, which come to us dried if at all, are said to be responsible, along with yogurt, for imparting extreme longevity. There are reports of people there living to 150 years.

Bananas are believed to impart wisdom, a fig tree provided shade to Buddha while he meditated his way to perfect knowledge, and melons took all of France by storm.

The melon "invaded France at the end of the fifteenth century," wrote Georges and Germaine Blond. "It was often called the *pompon*. Ronsard celebrated it many times under this name; a gardener proud of his produce, he offered some to Charles IX, a great lover of melons; Henri IV appreciated them no less: 'I am going to sit down at table to eat my melons and swallow a draft of muscat.' And Montaigne: 'I am not excessively fond of salads nor of fruits, except melons.' Melon was all the rage. 1583 even saw the appearance of a *Succinct Treatise on Melons* by the very serious Jacques Pons, dean of the college of Doctors of Lyons, which listed fifty ways of eating this fruit, as hors d'oeuvre, chilled, with sugar, salt or pepper, cooked in soups, in fritters and in compotes. Even the rind was used for compotes. Renaissance France smelled of melon."

The shape, color, fragrance and taste of fruits seem to appeal to us on many levels. Throughout the centuries artists have made fruits the subject of innumerable paintings, both as subjects on their own merits and as symbols for spiritual or immaterial concepts, and theological attributes. The taste and fragrance of a particular fruit enjoyed in childhood seems to remain a lifetime. From Henry James, ". . . the very air of long summer afternoons—occasions tasting of ample leisure, still bookless, yet beginning to be bedless, or cribless, tasting of accessible garden peaches . . ." And Henry Adams, ". . . summer was drunken. Among senses, smell was the strongest—smell of hot pine-woods and sweet-fern in the scorching summer noon; of new mown hay; of ploughed earth; of box hedges; of peaches, lilacs, syringas." Or Waverley Root, "My father cut down a magnificent plum tree which every year had given us a bountiful harvest of sweet juicy blue or red plums, I have forgotten which, and every second or third year, I have forgotten which again, a bumper crop, in order to make room for a backyard garage. The car it contained was only a Maxwell. A whole fleet of Rolls-Royces would not have compensated for the home-made fresh plum ice cream which disappeared with our tree."

Everyone has his favorite fruit and this too evokes in many writers a special response. Elizabeth David writes charmingly of hers: "The beautiful, aromatically-scented little golden fruit which is the apricot is one which I bracket with the fig as being the most elusive and most rare to find in perfect condition. To the fortunate it occurs every now and again to bite into the sweet purple flesh of a fig as it is ready to crack through its bright green skin or to pick the perfect ripe apricot warm from the sun. Then one sniffs and eats and is thankful that one should have been so favoured by Providence" *(French Provincial Cooking).*

William Butler declared unequivocally about the strawberry: "Doubtless God could have made a better berry, but doubtless God never did."

In various periods of history and in a great many different cuisines fruit has provided flavor to meats, poultry, even fish. It has appeared in stews, salads, soups, hearty cereals and breads. But always it has found its most important place, fulfilled its happiest function, and brought the greatest pleasure as the dessert course to bring completion to a rich and satisfying meal.

Except in summertime, most of the fruit we buy is picked and shipped while it is green and hard. It ripens on the road or not at all. Most fruit can use a little culinary help to make it tender and enhance its flavor. A pinch of spice, some herbs, some wine or brandy, sugar, and a little gentle poaching can work a miracle with rock-hard pears or almost any other fruit.

Nature can be infuriatingly indifferent to our convenience and desires. When ripe and fragrant fruit finally appears, after a long time, it comes at once, in quantity and briefly, only to disappear again. So every summer we are faced with overflowing baskets of fragile, ripe peaches, plums, apricots, nectarines . . . How many can we eat just as they are? How soon before they spoil? Surely not all. But plunge them into boiling water, peel and pit them, then poach in sugar syrup and they will last for several days, and make desserts fit for a king.

Stewed fruit, baked fruit, fools, puddings, compotes, fruits poached in syrups and in wine have been around for many hundred years, practiced by every housewife with access to an orchard. The great chef Auguste Escoffier invented a repertoire of luscious and lovely desserts based on fruit. Working for César Ritz in 1883 in Monte Carlo, Escoffier found himself faced with a then novel and intriguing challenge. Women were just beginning to dine publicly in restaurants, something that was unheard of except for certain types of ladies with no reputation to preserve. In an attempt to encourage the presence of more proper ladies, Ritz designed luxurious, beautifully lighted restaurants and Escoffier gave much thought to the kinds of dishes that ladies would find particularly appealing. Therefore desserts were most important as they came last and left the last impression. He named many of his most famous desserts in honor of great ladies of the operatic stage. Pêches Melba for Nellie Melba, poires Mary Garden for another operatic luminary, and poires Belle-Hélène for Gabrielle Réjane, the star of Offenbach's light opera, called *La Belle-Hélène.*

Of all these, pêches Melba may be the most famous and Escoffier wrote this account of how it came about: "Madame Nellie Melba, the *grande cantatrice* of Australia, sang at Covent Garden . . . in 1894. She stayed at the Savoy Hotel . . . at which time I was directing the kitchens of that important establishment. One evening, when Lohingrin (sic) was to be performed, Madame Melba gave me two seats in the orchestra. As you know, in that opera a swan appears. The following evening Madame Melba gave a *petit souper* for several friends, among them Monseigneur le Duc d'Orléans, and to show her that I had profited agreeably from the seats that she had graciously offered me, I sculpted in a block of ice a superb swan, and between the two wings I buried a silver bowl. I covered the bottom of the bowl with vanilla ice cream and on this bed of ice cream I placed peaches . . . soaked for several minutes in a syrup of vanilla . . . A purée of fresh raspberries covered the peaches completely. Thus deliciously completed, this dessert was to become world famous. . . ."

And so it has. Though most of us must do away with swans carved from ice, who can resist poached peaches topped with a raspberry purée?

FRUIT DESSERTS

Fruit to be served whole or raw should be of the best quality. Save overripe or damaged specimens for cooking or sauce making. Don't look for the largest specimens only. In some species these have lost flavor through the very plant breeding that made them larger. Color and shape may be poor indicators with other kinds. Remember how you plan to use the fruit. Unless you are going to make a large batch of sauce, or use fruit for canning or freezing, buy only small amounts. All fruits are perishable, and even if not spoiled or dried out they may lose flavor and nutrients in storage.

While all kinds of fruits are available all year long, imported from far reaches of the world, it is always best to buy fruit in season. Whenever possible buy fruit produced in your own area, since it will have a shorter trip from orchard to market and will be fresher, less likely to be bruised and more likely to be nearly ripe.

When you get your fruit home, look it over and gently brush off any soil. Since moisture may encourage decay wash just before using. If the fruits are not ripe, place them in a single layer in a rather shadowy spot at room temperature; do not put them in sunlight or direct light. Check on them every day; do not let them become too soft or show wrinkled skin. If they do not ripen in a reasonable time, they may have been picked too green; use them for cooking, as the flavor will be disappointing.

If the fruits are ripe, refrigerate them; the only exception is bananas, which turn brown and mushy under refrigeration. If you buy fruits in plastic bags, unpack them; if left all bunched together, one damaged specimen could spoil the rest. Even in the re-frigerator try to space them out so they are not touching.

All fruits taste sweeter and have the best of their true flavor when at room temperature. If you have stored them in a refrigerator or cold room, bring them to room temperature before serving. Allow 20 minutes to 1 hour, depending on the size. Berries will need the smallest amount of time. The exceptions are mixtures of fruits with cream and gelatin.

As soon as fruits are peeled and cut, they begin to dry and to lose vitamins by oxidation. Apples and pears begin to discolor. The simplest step to preserve color is to brush fruit with a mixture of lemon juice and water. Other citrus juices can also be used. To serve with more flourish, add grated rind and a little rum, Cointreau, Grand Marnier, kirsch or Cognac. Simple desserts can be made by covering prepared fruits with red or white wine.

Fruits and Cheese

Cheese enhances the flavor of many of the fruits we like to eat out of hand.

Serve Crema Danica with cherries. Serve Camembert, provolone, Appenzeller or Pont l'Évêque with grapes. Sheep's-milk and goat's-milk cheeses such as feta are also good with grapes; goat's-milk cheeses such

Puréeing Fruit

1 Put fresh, frozen or cooked fruit into container of electric blender.

2 Purée on medium speed for approximately 30 seconds. Strain through sieve if required.

OR Put fruit in work bowl of processor.

3 Process for 10 seconds or until smooth texture is reached.

Combining Purée and Cream

as chèvre are delicious with figs. Brie and nectarines, Gorgonzola and peaches, Roquefort and pears—all are delicious combinations. Triple cream cheeses such as Gervais or Chantilly are good with apricots, strawberries or peaches. Stilton is good with purple plums, and Appenzeller goes well with red plums. All types of Cheddar cheeses are harmonious with apples, both raw and cooked.

Fruit Purées

Since fruits are naturally juicy, many of them can be puréed raw. All soft fruits and very ripe fruits in good shape can be puréed, to be used fresh in fruit soups, snows, whips, fools, mousses, crèmes and ice creams, as well as fruit sauces, and can be frozen to add a touch of summer to winter meals. Soft fruit purées are not only nutritious, they are very easy to make.

Wash fruit carefully, peel if necessary, and cut out any damaged or bruised parts. Place small quantities in a blender or food processor fitted with the steel blade. Purée the fruit, then sieve or put through a food mill to remove any fibers or seeds. Sweeten purée with sugar to taste. Use granular or superfine sugar, and be sure it is completely dissolved in the purée.

Harder fruits need cooking, but any fruit can be cooked if you wish. Prepare them as for raw fruit purées, then cut large fruits into small pieces.

Cook in the smallest possible amount of water over low heat, until fruit is very soft. Use a skimmer to transfer fruit to sieve or mill, so that the purée is not too wet. Save the liquid; you may need to add a little for perfect texture, or the juices can be used in fruit sauces.

When it comes to puréeing the cooked fruit, certain fruits are best suited to specific methods:

The food mill is best for tree fruits (apples, pears, apricots, peaches, cherries).

A sieve can be used for soft fruits such as strawberries. All berries need either sieve or mill to remove seeds.

1 Wash and prepare fruit. Stew or poach if necessary. Drain well.

2 Purée fruit for creams, snows, whips or mousses; crush with a fork for fools and custards.

3 For a custard, stir in cold thick custard. Cream may be added later to give a marbled effect.

4 For a cream, fold whipped cream into puréed fruit, cutting and folding so cream does not lose air.

Using Fruit Purées

Fruit purées, either raw or cooked, can be combined with whipped cream, beaten egg whites, custard or cream cheese to make delicate desserts.

A fool is a mixture of fruit and whipped cream only. While puréed fruit can be used for a fool, it should properly be crushed rather than puréed, so that all the fruit juices blend with the cream and the dessert keeps a rough texture. The fruit may be raw or cooked. You will need 1 cup crushed fruit to 1 cup heavy cream; the cream will double when whipped.

A whip is a mixture of sweetened purée with beaten egg whites or whipped cream.

A cream (or crème) is made with puréed raw fruit mixed with whipped cream or cream cheese, or some of both. Part of the cream may be sour cream, or evaporated milk can be whipped to replace cream.

Custards use less fruit, about one third fruit to two thirds custard; the fruit is often crushed rather than puréed. Whipped cream can be carefully folded in at the end to lighten the mixture and give a rich marbling effect.

When crushing fruit for fools or custards, do it in a bowl large enough for the rest of the ingredients. In this way no juice is lost. Crush fruit, raw or cooked, with a fork or potato masher, but stop short of mashing it, for the fruit should add a rough texture to the finished dish.

Cream for these desserts should be whipped to soft peaks, not whipped stiff. When cream is folded into the

Sautéing and Flaming Fruits

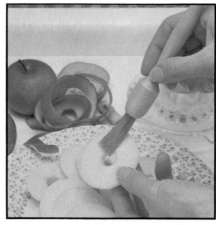

1 Prepare the fruit. If flaming it, pour the spirit into a small pan.

2 Melt most of the butter in a large frying pan over heat.

4 Brown the fruit slices on both sides. Turn carefully with a spatula and a round-bladed knife.

5 Remove fruit with a spatula, allowing excess butter to fall back into the pan. Keep fruit warm.

6 Add more butter to pan if necessary and cook remaining slices of fruit.

8 Return all fruit to the pan and sprinkle or spoon the sweetener over it.

9 Ignite the spirit, stand well back, and pour the flaming spirit over the fruit.

10 Let flames die completely. Transfer the fruit to a warmed serving dish.

Put in as many slices of fruit as will fit in a single layer.

7 Warm the spirit by setting the small pan over low heat. Never allow it to boil.

11 Scatter chopped nuts, dried or candied fruit on top. Add cream or serve it separately.

cool base, it becomes stiffer. And if cream is stiff to start with, it can separate as it is folded into the fruit and the dessert can taste buttery. The fruit or other base must be cold or the cream will melt into liquid again.

Chill the finished fruit dessert in a large glass bowl or in individual serving dishes for about 1 hour, but try to serve it then, for without gelatin the mixture may start to separate if stored too long. At serving time you may wish to decorate the dessert with shreds of candied peel or angelica; whole perfect fruits that match the purée or combine well with it; sautéed almond slivers or chopped hazelnuts or walnuts; a single mint leaf.

Shallow-Frying or Sautéing Fruits

Shallow-frying is a quick and easy way to turn the contents of your fruit bowl into a delicious hot dessert. It is an excellent method for turning underripe and hard fruits into luscious dishes. Slices of fruit can be sautéed quickly in butter so they still keep their shape and stay firm but are heated through and become slightly softened in texture. The color is brightened and the sugar or other sweetener makes an attractive glaze.

Sautéed fruits can be served simply sweetened, or they can be flamed with a spirit or fortified wine, to make a special dish.

There are only a few fruits suitable for shallow-frying, those with a firm structure such as apples and peaches, or those held together with membranes such as citrus fruits.

Apples. Use crisp eating apples; cooking apples prepared this way will usually be too tart. Prepare 4 large or 6 small apples to serve 4 people. Peel and core apples, then cut them into ½-inch slices or rings, or quarter and divide into lengthwise slices. If you prepare them more than 10 minutes in advance, brush all unpeeled surfaces with lemon juice to prevent discoloration.

Bananas. Use firm, slightly underripe bananas with no brown speckles. Allow 1 banana per person. Peel them and cut lengthwise into halves. For ease in handling, you can also cut each piece crosswise.

Pineapples. Use firm fruit, not overripe, with a good color all over. Prepare 1 medium-size or large pineapple for 4 people.

Peaches and Nectarines. Use very firm fruit, just ripe but not green-tinged. Prepare 1 large or 2 small peaches or nectarines per person. Scald and peel the peaches, but leave the skin on nectarines. Halve and pit either fruit; they may be sautéed as halves, or can be cut lengthwise into ¼-inch-thick slices.

Oranges and Grapefruits. These are delicious shallow-fried. Prepare 1 large orange or 1 medium-size grapefruit per person. Cut away the

Shallow-Frying or Sautéing Fruits

Fruit	Temperature under pan	Total cooking time in minutes
Apples	high	1½
Bananas	moderate	3½
Oranges and Grapefruits	high	1½
Peaches and Nectarines	high	1½
Pineapples	high	2½

rind and the white portion of the peel completely. Cut the fruit into ½-inch slices and pick out the seeds and the white center of each slice.

Butter. Fruit is always sautéed in butter for best flavor and color. Clarified unsalted butter is best, as there is no danger of it burning. However, raw butter, salted or unsalted, can be used. You will need about 3 tablespoons butter for 1 pound of fruit.

Sweeteners and Spices. All fruits can be sweetened with sugar. Granulated sugar, or sugars flavored with vanilla or cinnamon, give a light brown glaze. Dark brown sugar gives a darker glaze. Honey also goes well with all fruits.

Melted red-currant jelly is delicious with peaches and nectarines. Try a jam or jelly of a different flavor to go with your chosen fruit: apricot jam with pineapple, for example. Marmalade can be used with apples. As a rough guide, you will need 3 to 4 tablespoons sugar, jam, jelly or marmalade to sweeten 1 pound of fruit, or 2 to 3 tablespoons honey.

A little spice such as a pinch of grated nutmeg or ground cinnamon can be added with the sweetener.

Toppings. To make these sautéed fruits even more attractive, garnish them with a tasty topping, or serve them with cream. Add the toppings just before serving the fruits. Prepare them in advance so they are ready when the fruit dish is to be served.

Scatter any of the following over the fruit: chopped nuts, sesame seeds, sunflower seeds, chopped candied peel or angelica, sliced glacé cherries, dried currants, dark or light raisins. Spoon blobs of whipped cream on top. Do not attempt to pipe cream in shapes on the hot fruit, as it will melt at once. The cream mingling with the fruit juices makes a delicious sauce. Alternately, serve cream, sour cream or yogurt separately.

If no spices have been used in cooking the fruit, grate a little nutmeg or sprinkle a little cinnamon over the cream.

Equipment. You will need a large heavy frying pan, a spatula and a round-bladed knife to turn the fruit, and a plate on which to keep it warm if you have to cook the fruit in batches.

Flaming Fruits

When sautéed fruit is flamed, all the excess fat in the pan and also the alcohol in the spirit or fortified wine is burned up. The color of the fruit is heightened and the sauce that remains is rich and clear.

Any spirit can be used to flame fruits. Do not use old alcohol that has been in the cupboard for a long time, as its flaming quality will be much reduced. The most popular spirits are plain brandy or the special brandy from Cognac, Calvados or American apple brandy (applejack), rum and kirsch. It is possible to use whiskey, vodka or tequila. Liqueurs make a sweeter dish. Grand Marnier and other orange-flavored liqueurs are good with dishes containing orange, but they blend well with all fruits. The coffee-flavored liqueurs are delicious with pineapple.

Fortified wines can be used if they have not been opened for too long a time. Their alcohol content is lower and so evaporates more quickly than that in spirits or liqueurs. Use sherry, port, Madeira, Marsala, Malaga, or the sweet fortified wines of France if you can find them in your markets.

How to Flame Fruits. There are two ways to add the alcohol. It may be warmed, poured on the fruit, and ignited. However, the alcohol may disperse in the juice and sugar too quickly so that it will not ignite. The other method is to warm the alcohol, ignite it, and pour it flaming onto the fruit. If you are following the second method, be sure to clear anything flammable from the area where you are working, especially above the pan.

Melt butter in the frying pan, add the fruit in a single layer, and brown slices on both sides. Turn the slices so they brown evenly, using a spatula and a round-bladed knife. Do not try to flip the fruit over with a single implement, and do not turn the fruit more than twice or it may begin to break up. Re-

Broiling Fruits

1 Preheat broiler to medium. Place broiler pan or rack 4 inches below the source of heat.

OR Warm honey in a heavy pan. Add flavorings and spread honey over fruit with a pastry brush.

move browned fruit to a plate, add more butter if needed, and continue until all the fruit is done. Return all the slices to the frying pan and sprinkle on the sugar and any flavoring.

Heat the alcohol in a small shallow pan. Light a long match and hold it above the liquid at the side of the pan to ignite it. Stand well back and pour the flaming spirit over the fruit. Do not hold the handle of the frying pan; the flames will be really high for a few minutes. Let the flames die completely. Transfer the fruit and all its sticky sauce to a warmed serving dish. Decorate just before serving. Flaming can be done at table, pro-

2 Prepare the fruit. Melt a little butter and brush it over the fruit.

OR Soak the fruit in liquid, such as ginger syrup or wine, for 30 minutes before broiling. Drain.

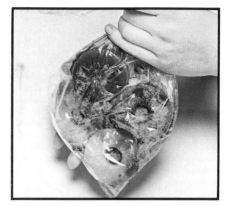

3 Put some brown sugar in a plastic bag. Add fruit and shake. Shake off excess sugar.

4 Arrange fruit in a shallow flameproof dish on the broiler rack and broil until the surface is golden.

5 Turn, using a spatula and a round-bladed knife to avoid breaking the fruit.

6 Broil the other side until golden and bubbling. Remove from the broiler and serve immediately.

vided all safety precautions are followed. In that case, transfer the heated fruit to a shallow flameproof dish before pouring in the flaming spirit.

Broiling and Baking Fruit

Broiling and baking give delightful appearance and flavor to cooked fruit in surprisingly little time.

Broiling is both quick and effective. It cooks the surface of the fruit and heats it through without destroying the flavor and freshness. Because it is a quick method, broiling is an ideal way to give new appearance and flavor to canned fruit as well as being an excellent way to serve juicy fresh fruit.

Baking is a good method for the cook pressed for time because once the fruit has been prepared it needs no further attention. Baking can also be an economical use of energy as the fruit can be baked in the oven at the same time as a casserole or roast.

Both methods lend themselves to simple and elegant dishes. Bananas, for instance, can be broiled *à la Beauharnaise,* with white rum and cream, or economically with brown sugar, lemon juice and raisins. You can make both sweet or savory dishes. On the simplest level, baked apples can be turned into a supper or luncheon dish by stuffing them with a meat or fish filling instead of the usual sugar and raisins. Broiled and baked fruits can be used to enhance roasts and broiled meats. Try broiled pineapple rings with sausages, hamburgers, frankfurters, ham or chicken. Try broiled or baked apples with duck, pork or lamb, and broiled bananas with fried chicken or ham.

To prepare fruits for broiling and baking you will need a sharp knife, a swivel peeler, a grapefruit knife, an ap-

84

ple corer, and a grooved board or a plate to catch juices when fruits are being cut.

Broiling Fruits

This method takes only 5 minutes at the most. As it cooks only the surface of the fruit, it is suitable only for fruits that can be eaten raw.

The fruit must be sliced or halved. Apples are cored and cut into rings. Large apples are best. The slices should be about ½ inch thick. Peeling is optional. Apricots and peaches are peeled, halved, and pitted. Oranges and grapefruits are prepared as for breakfast grapefruit. Oranges may also be sliced. Pineapple should be cut into ½-inch-thick slices. Bananas are peeled and cut lengthwise into halves.

To prevent fruit drying under the broiler, it must be moistened with melted butter. When broiling apples and bananas, it is wise to brush with butter immediately after cutting to prevent browning. For extra flavor, grated nutmeg or ground ginger or cinnamon can be added to the butter. For special occasions, try soaking the fruit in syrup from a jar of preserved ginger, or in brandy, wine or fruit juice. About 1 hour of soaking will let the fruit absorb flavor and moisture.

Adding sweetener is not essential, as most of the fruits used are already sweet, but adding brown sugar or honey gives an attractive caramelized appearance. In the case of cooking apples, a sweetener is essential. Fruit slices can be tossed in brown sugar. Place sugar in a plastic bag, add the fruit, a few slices or pieces at a time, and shake until coated. Remove fruit and shake excess sugar back into the bag for the next batch.

If using honey, warm it a little or dip a knife into boiling water and spread honey over both sides of the fruit. About 2 tablespoons liquid honey will coat 12 slices of fruit. To sweeten peaches and apricots, simply fill the cavity with brown sugar, honey or jelly. Black- and red-currant jelly are good for this.

How to Broil Fruits. Heat the broiler to moderate and place the pan or rack about 4 inches below the heat source. Place the prepared fruit on a flameproof dish and set the dish on the pan or rack. It is better to cook the fruit in a dish as it is easier to spoon the juices out of the dish than out of a broiler pan. Broil for no more than 5 minutes, just long enough to turn the surface golden. When cooking slices, turn them over as soon as one side becomes golden. As broiled fruit is quite soft, do not use tongs, but slip a spatula underneath the slice, place a round-bladed knife on top, and turn.

Always serve broiled fruit as soon as it is cooked. If kept waiting, it will overcook and lose its delicious fresh flavor.

Baking Fruits

Baking is a slow method, but it has the advantage of cooking the fruit without destroying the shape. Fruits are usually baked in an uncovered dish.

Fruits for baking can be whole, or halved .and stuffed. Apples may be cored, peeled or not peeled, whole, halved or quartered, or stuffed. Peeling for stuffing is not advisable as the skin helps to keep the fruit in shape. Pears and quinces should be peeled and cored; they may be left whole, halved or quartered. Apricots and peaches should be peeled, halved, and pitted. Bananas can be baked with their skins on, or can be peeled and left whole. Plums may be halved and pitted, or they can be left whole and can be slit around the natural indentation to prevent bursting.

To prevent drying and sticking, hard fruits such as apples, pears and quinces should be baked with liquid, enough to come about halfway up the sides of the fruit pieces in the case of apples, and to cover the pieces in the case of pears and quinces. This liquid can be water, sweet syrup (see the chart for Syrups for Poaching), wine, cider or fruit juice. Apricots, peaches and bananas should be baked in a well-buttered dish, except when bananas are baked in their skins. For an extra buttery taste, fruit can be dotted with

Baking Fruits

Fruit	Preparation	Time in minutes
Apples	whole	60
	whole, stuffed	45
	halved	40
	quartered	35
Apricots		30
Bananas	in skins	30
	peeled	20
Peaches		15
Pears	whole	45 to 90
	halved	40 to 50
	quartered	35 to 45
Quinces	whole	2 to 2¾ hours
	halved	1½ to 2 hours
	quartered	1 to 1½ hours

The range of time for pears and quinces depends on the ripeness of the fruits.

butter, which melts and forms a sauce with the fruit juices.

For stuffed fruit, the sweetener is included in the stuffing. Make the stuffing very sweet and scatter any extra around the fruit to form a sauce with the liquid. Whole or quartered pears and quinces should always be baked with a sweet syrup. The best way to sweeten apricots and peaches is to fill the pit cavities with sugar, honey, jam or jelly. Blackberry and red-currant jelly are excellent. Sprinkle bananas with brown sugar or spread with honey. Bananas are naturally sweet, so use only a thin covering of sweetener.

How to Bake Fruits. Preheat oven to 350°F. Prepare the fruit and arrange on a suitable baking dish. If other foods are being baked in the oven at a higher temperature, place the fruit dish on the bottom of the oven. The time needed depends on the degree of ripeness or the natural hardness of the fruit. The chart for Baking Fruits gives guidelines. Generally speaking, the fruit is cooked when it can be pierced easily with a very thin skewer or even better with a large sewing needle, which makes so small a

Stewing Fruits

hole it will not be apparent when the fruit is served. If in doubt after that, slice off a tiny piece and eat it.

Stewing and Poaching Fruits

Fruit that is underripe or naturally sharp in flavor (rhubarb, quinces, cooking apples) is unpleasant to eat raw but is ideal for stewing or poaching. When cooked with care, stewed and poached fruits retain their shape and are juicy and sweet. Fruits prepared this way are delicious served hot with a sweet sauce or cold with ice cream or heavy cream. They are also excellent and decorative arranged in a spongecake, pastry or biscuit crust. They also provide the basis for many puddings such as charlottes, crumbles, fools and cobblers.

Stewed and poached fruits are often served with meat and fish. Classic examples are applesauce with pork, cranberry sauce with duck or turkey, red currants with lamb or venison, peaches with ham, and gooseberries with mackerel.

These fruits are excellent for breakfast, providing a refreshing and nutritious start for the day.

A sweetener is always added for stewing and poaching, and sometimes complementary flavors are added. Measure these ingredients carefully for good results. Both processes can be done on top of the stove or in the oven. The cooking should be gentle so the fruit does not disintegrate in either method. Cooking at high heat will reduce the fruit to shapeless pulp, which may taste delicious but will look disappointing.

In stewing, liquid and sweetener are added separately; in poaching, liquid and sweetener are first cooked together to make a syrup, and the fruit is added when the syrup is ready.

You will need a heavy pan or casserole with a tight-fitting lid for both methods. Covering the pan is important because it prevents loss of moisture and flavor. A heavy pan is important for even distribution of the heat. Good-quality heavy aluminum or stainless steel saucepans with a sand-

1 pound fruit
¾ cup sugar, or 2 tablespoons honey
¼ cup fruit juice, wine, cider, water, or a mixture of water with one of the other liquids
additional flavorings (optional)

1 Prepare the fruit. Small fruits can be left whole; large fruits should be peeled, cored and sliced before cooking.

2 Put fruit in a heavy saucepan or casserole. Add half of sweetener plus chosen liquid and any flavorings.

3 Cover the saucepan or casserole and cook over gentle heat. Stir occasionally.

4 Halfway through cooking, taste fruit and add remaining sweetener if needed.

5 Toward end of cooking, test fruit with a skewer or needle, or eat a berry. If fruit is tender, it is cooked.

wich base (aluminum between layers of stainless steel) are ideal. A flameproof casserole of enameled cast iron is excellent for use in the oven.

On top of the stove use very low heat so the fruit is just simmering. If you are obliged to use a thin-based pan, place an asbestos pad between pan and heat. For fruit to be cooked in the oven, the temperature should be about 350°F. A shallow casserole makes it possible to arrange the pieces of fruit in a single layer.

Citrus fruits, strawberries, melons, pineapples and grapes are too watery to stew or poach. Most other fruits are excellent, but cooking apples, rhubarb, green gooseberries, blackberries, currants, loganberries and raspberries are better stewed than poached. Harder fruits and fruits cooked in their skins such as cherries, cooking pears, quinces, peaches, apricots, plums, damsons and greengages, are better poached, as this method allows them to release juices but still retain their shape.

You will need an apple corer, a sharp stainless-steel knife, a cherry pitter, a cutting board, a colander, and a swivel peeler for peeling apples, pears and quinces.

Making Simple Syrup

1 Put 1¼ cups water, 1¼ cups granulated sugar and 1 teaspoon lemon juice in a saucepan. Stir to dissolve sugar completely.

2 Place pan over medium heat and bring to a boil, stirring all the time with a wooden spoon.

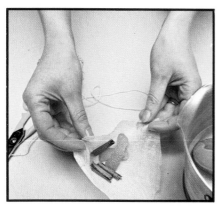

3 Boil rapidly for 2 minutes. Remove from heat and add flavorings, tied in a muslin bag if necessary.

4 When syrup is cold, pour it over prepared fruit. Chill to blend flavors, then warm up a little before serving.

Syrups for Fruit

Sugar Syrups are excellent, beginning with the syrup from already cooked fruits or that from candied gingerroot. Your own syrups can be made and stored in covered jars to be ready when needed.

Syrups for Poaching Fruits (based on 1 pound fruit and 1 cup water)

Fruit	Sugar in cups	Honey in tablespoons
Apricots	¾	1
Cherries	1	1½
Cranberries	1¾	3
Gooseberries	1	1½
Peaches	¾	1
Pears	1	1½
Plums	1	1½
Quinces	1	1½

Apples, Pears and Quinces. All these fruits should be peeled and cored. Quarter apples for poaching or slice for stewing. Leave pears whole, or halve or quarter for poaching. However, for some recipes pears may be cooked without peeling, or may retain their stems. Quinces may be cooked whole, halved or quartered.

Rhubarb. The green leaves of rhubarb are poisonous because of their high content of oxalic acid. Cut them off completely. Trim the root end of each stalk. Early or hothouse rhubarb is tender so there is no need to peel it. Garden rhubarb has rather tough skin that should be removed with a sharp knife before cooking, although the cooked fruit will be less pretty; the pink color is in the skin, and without it the stewed fruit is mostly green. Cut stalks into 1-inch lengths.

Berries. Wash gooseberries, raspberries, cranberries, currants and blackberries, and discard any little stems or bits of leaf. Do not let the berries soak, but wash quickly.

Peaches, Apricots, Cherries.

Poaching Fruits

Peel peaches and apricots, halve them, and pit them. Pit the cherries.

Plums. Wash and leave whole, or halve and pit. If left whole, they must be pricked with a fork or skewer before cooking or they will burst. Alternately, cut a slit around the natural curve of the fruit; it will fall into halves during cooking and the pit comes out easily.

How to Stew Fruits. Stew fruit in a minimum of liquid, just enough to cover the bottom of the pan and keep the fruit from sticking or burning before it releases enough juices of its own. Use only a few spoonfuls of liquid. If too much is used, the liquid must be boiled after the fruit has been lifted out, to reduce it and concentrate the flavor. The liquid can be water, fresh fruit juice, cider or wine, or equal quantities of water and one of the other liquids.

Sweetening is needed to make most cooked fruit palatable. Use white or brown sugar or honey. The amount depends on the tartness of the fruit. Start with half the amount called for in a recipe and add more halfway through the cooking if fruit does not seem sweet enough. When stewing plums, do not add any sweetener until half-cooked because sugar tends to toughen the skins.

Extra flavorings such as orange or lemon rind or spices can be added.

Put prepared fruit and liquid in a heavy pan. Sprinkle in half of the sweetener and any flavoring. Place pan over low heat and cook gently. To ensure even cooking and prevent sticking, occasionally stir the contents. If you are cooking berries, a spoon might bruise or break the fruit, so shake the pan instead, holding the lid firmly in one hand and the handle in the other.

Taste for sweetness about halfway through cooking time and add more sugar or honey as needed. Test the fruit by pricking with a thin skewer or large sewing needle. Or lift out a berry and eat it. If the fruit is done, it will offer no resistance to the skewer or your teeth.

Very juicy fruits such as rhubarb, currants, blackberries and raspberries can be stewed without any liquid because their naturally high water con-

¾ cup sugar, or 2 tablespoons honey
1 cup water
1 teaspoon lemon juice
1 pound prepared fruit
    additional flavorings (optional)

1 Place sweetener, water and lemon juice in a heavy saucepan. Stir once, then bring to a boil, stirring. Boil for 2 minutes.

2 Remove syrup from heat. Add flavorings. Carefully lower the prepared fruit into the syrup.

OR Place prepared fruit in an oven-proof dish. Add flavorings to the syrup and pour it over the fruit.

3 Cover container and cook over gentle heat or bake at 350°F, basting occasionally, until fruit is tender.

3 If poaching on top of stove, carefully lift cooked fruit from syrup to a serving dish. Pour syrup over it.

Best Methods of Stewing and Poaching Fruits

Fruit	Stewing on Stove in minutes	Poaching on Stove in minutes	Stewing or Poaching in 350°F Oven in minutes
Apples quartered		15	25
sliced	10 to 12		20
Apricots		10 to 20	25 to 30
Blackberries	10		15 to 20
Cherries		20 to 30	25 to 40
Cranberries	10		15 to 20
Currants	10		15 to 20
Gooseberries		20 to 30	25 to 40
Peaches		15 to 20	25 to 30
Pears whole		40	50 to 70
halved		30	40 to 50
quartered		25	35
Plums whole		15 to 20	25 to 30
halved		10 to 15	20 to 25
Raspberries	10		12 to 15
Quinces whole		1 to 2 hours	2 to 3 hours
halved		1 to 1½ hours	2 to 2½ hours
quartered		about 1 hour	1½ to 2 hours
Rhubarb	10 to 15		20 to 25

The range of time depends on the ripeness of the fruits.

tent makes additional liquid unnecessary. Simply sprinkle the pan of fruit with sugar and flavorings and cook.

Although rhubarb is juicy, it takes a little time to release any juice because the outer skin is not porous. For this one fruit, the best method is to put rhubarb slices in a pan with sugar and flavoring about 1 hour before cooking so that the juice begins to be drawn out before cooking begins.

Another way to stew fruit is by the French method, which uses butter in place of liquid. This is particularly good for apples. Allow 4 tablespoons butter for each pound of fruit.

How to Poach Fruits. Make a sugar syrup, and be sure to get the degree of sweetness right at the start. Consult the chart for Syrups for suitable amounts of syrup for various fruits. Add flavorings to the syrup after it has been boiled. Use a cinnamon stick for pears, quinces, apples, rhubarb, peaches and apricots; remove cinnamon stick before serving fruit. Vanilla is excellent with all fruits; add a vanilla bean when making the syrup, or use vanilla sugar for the sweetener in the syrup (to make vanilla sugar, bury a bean in a jar of granulated or confectioners' sugar). Ground cardamom combined with orange rind or an orange-flavored liqueur such as Curaçao is delicious with pears and quinces. Chopped crystallized or preserved gingerroot is good with rhubarb, pears, peaches, apricots, plums and apples. A suitable spirit adds extra flavor; add it to the syrup after it has been boiled, before pouring syrup over the fruit. Just a few drops will serve. Try kirsch with apricots and cherries, rum with pears, brandy with peaches.

If you are poaching fruit on top of the stove, remove the syrup pan from the heat before adding the fruit, to avoid splashing the hot syrup and burning yourself. Cover pan with a lid and return to the heat. Poach at a gentle simmer, occasionally spooning syrup over the fruit or turning it over if it is not completely immersed in syrup.

Poaching fruit in the oven results in more even cooking because heat surrounds the pan on all sides. This method is easier for beginners; place the fruit in the ovenproof dish and pour the syrup over it. If the dish can be used for serving, so much the better; you will not have to transfer the fruit from pan to dish and thus you avoid the danger of breaking it up in the process. Test poached fruit for doneness in the same fashion as stewed fruit.

Suggestions for Stewed and Poached Fruits

• Stew apples and cranberries together. The cranberries turn the apples rosy pink.

• Pit 1 pound cherries, cover with red wine, add 1 cup sugar and a pinch of cinnamon, and simmer gently for 10 minutes. Remove cherries and reduce liquid to a syrup by boiling rapidly for 2 minutes. Add 1 tablespoon currant jelly and let it melt. Pour syrup over cherries and serve with cream.

• Stew blackberries, red currants, black currants and cranberries and serve with yogurt or sour cream.

• Make quince and apple compote. Cook quinces first and add apples toward end of cooking time. Flavor with whole cloves and ground ginger.

• For quick fruit crumble, sprinkle warm stewed or poached fruit with crushed cookies. Particularly good are gooseberries or rhubarb with ginger cookies. Nuts can be added with the cookies.

• For aniseed apples, stew apples with ½ teaspoon whole aniseeds. Serve cold with whipped cream.

• Stew complementary fruits together, such as apples and blackberries, pears and plums; work out the timing carefully, adding those that need the shortest cooking time last.

• Sprinkle cooked fruit with chopped nuts; serve with light or heavy cream, or fluffy whipped cream, lightly sweetened with vanilla sugar.

Toffee Apples

4 portions

4   large or 6 small crisp
      eating apples
4   tablespoons butter

1   cup granulated sugar
      vanilla ice cream
      freshly grated nutmeg

Peel and core the apples and cut into ½-inch rings. Melt the butter in a large skillet over low heat. Add 2 tablespoons water and the sugar. Stir until the syrup turns caramel color. Put in the apple rings and simmer them gently for 2 minutes, until they are soft and the syrup has formed a sticky sauce. Transfer apples and sauce to 4 warmed serving bowls. Quickly put a portion of ice cream on top of each one and grate a little nutmeg over the top.

Baked Apples

4 portions

4   cooking apples (Rome
      Beauty, for example)
¼   cup raisins

1   cup brown sugar, or 2
      tablespoons honey
4   tablespoons butter

Preheat oven to 350°F. Wash and core the apples. Using a sharp knife, make an incision around the skins of the apples about halfway down. This keeps the skin from splitting and the apples from bursting during cooking. Mix raisins with brown sugar.

Butter an ovenproof dish with 2 tablespoons of the butter. Place apples in the dish. Using a teaspoon, pile the raisins and sugar into the core cavities. Scatter any leftover raisins around the apples. Pour in just enough water to reach ½ inch up the sides of the apples. Dot apples with remaining butter. Bake for 40 to 60 minutes, depending on size, until apples are tender when pierced with a thin skewer.

Variations: Instead of sugar and raisins, try any of the following fillings. For honeyed apples: mix 3 tablespoons chopped walnuts with 4 tablespoons honey; garnish the baked apples with walnut halves. For Norwegian apples: core the apples and bake without stuffing; halve and seed 4 ounces black grapes and divide 3 small tangerines into segments; chop the fruit and pile into the core cavities of the baked apples; top each apple with a scoop of vanilla ice cream. For Orlando apples: stuff them with chunky orange marmalade. For Christmas apples: stuff with mincemeat well fortified with brandy. For Pagoda apples: stuff with chopped crystallized or stem ginger mixed with 3 tablespoons brown sugar. For Damascus apples: stuff with 2 ounces chopped dates mixed with 2 tablespoons honey. For golden apples: stuff with a mixture of golden raisins and chopped hazelnuts.

Brandied Apples

4 portions

6 small or 4 large eating apples	½ cup heavy cream
3 tablespoons butter	½ teaspoon ground cinnamon
½ cup Cognac or Calvados	¼ cup brown sugar

Peel and core the apples and cut them into ½-inch-thick rounds. Heat half of the butter in a large skillet over high heat. Put in as many apple slices as will fit in a single layer and brown them on both sides, turning carefully. Remove apples and keep warm. Add more butter to the pan if necessary and brown remaining apples.

While the apples are being sautéed, pour the Cognac or Calvados into a small pan and warm over low heat. Pour the cream into a bowl and whip until soft peaks form. Return all apples to the skillet and sprinkle cinnamon and brown sugar over them. Ignite the warmed spirit, stand well back, and pour it over the apple rings. Let the flames die. Transfer warmed apples to a serving dish and top with blobs of whipped cream.

Spicy French Apples

4 portions

1 pound cooking apples	2 whole cloves
4 tablespoons butter	5 ounces mixed dried fruits
½ teaspoon ground cinnamon	2 ounces shelled hazelnuts, walnuts or almonds
¼ cup soft brown sugar	
½ lemon	

Peel and core the apples and cut into thin slices. Put them in a heavy saucepan or casserole and add the butter, cinnamon and 2 tablespoons of the sugar. Grate the lemon rind and add it to the apples. Cut a slice from the lemon and stud the sides with the cloves. Add the lemon slice to the apples. Cover the pan and stew apples gently over low heat for 5 minutes. Stir occasionally to prevent sticking and encourage even cooking. Test for sweetness and add remaining sugar as required, bearing in mind that the dried fruits will add extra sweetness. Continue cooking for 10 minutes longer, then stir in the dried fruits.

After 2 minutes, test the apples with the point of a knife. If tender, remove saucepan from the heat. Discard the clove-studded slice of lemon. Stir in the nuts just before serving.

Bananas in Orange Juice

4 portions

4 ripe but firm bananas	1 tablespoon brown sugar
2 ounces shelled walnuts	pinch of grated nutmeg
2 tablespoons butter	½ cup orange juice

Peel the bananas and cut them lengthwise into halves. Chop the walnuts. Melt the butter in a large skillet over moderate heat. Lay the bananas in the pan, cut side up, and brown the underside, about 1½ minutes. Sprinkle fruit with half of the sugar and turn them over. Sprinkle with remaining sugar and the nutmeg. Pour in the orange juice and cook for 2 minutes more. Transfer the bananas and pan juices to a warmed serving dish and scatter the walnuts over the bananas.

Variations: For bananas in rum, a traditional West Indian dish, replace orange juice with rum. Warm the rum. Cook bananas and sugar for 1½ minutes only, then ignite the rum and pour it flaming over the bananas. Let the flames die before transferring bananas to a warmed serving dish.

Bananas à la Beauharnaise

4 portions

2 tablespoons butter	¼ cup rum
4 ripe but firm bananas	5 or 6 macaroons
2 tablespoons brown sugar	½ cup heavy cream

Preheat broiler to medium and coat a shallow flameproof dish with the butter. Peel the bananas and place in the buttered dish. Sprinkle with brown sugar. Pour the rum over the bananas. Heat gently on top of the stove for 5 minutes. Meanwhile, put the macaroons in a plastic bag and crush with a rolling pin.

Place the bananas under the broiler 4 inches from the source of heat. Broil for 4 minutes, until the sugar bubbles. Pour the cream over the bananas and sprinkle the macaroons on top.

Bananas Foster

6 portions

4 ripe but firm bananas	1 tablespoon banana liqueur
4 tablespoons butter	3 tablespoons brandy
6 tablespoons brown sugar	1 pint vanilla ice cream

Peel the bananas and slice them lengthwise into halves. Melt the butter and sugar in a large skillet over moderate heat, stirring frequently. When the sugar is completely melted, lay the bananas in the pan and cook 5 to 7 minutes, or until tender. Add the banana liqueur and stir.

Meanwhile pour the brandy into a small pan and warm it over low heat. Ignite the brandy and pour over the bananas. When the flames die down, serve over vanilla ice cream.

Compote of Dried Fruits

A compote is a dish of fruit, fresh or dried, cooked in a syrup flavored with aromatics such as cinnamon, cloves or lemon peel. A simple compote contains one kind of fruit, while others contain several fruits. A compote is usually served cold and is often sprinkled with a liqueur, such as kirsch, before serving.

6 to 8 portions

4 cups mixed dried fruits (apples, apricots, light and dark raisins, prunes, etc.)	¾ cup dry red wine
	1 cup sugar
	1 cinnamon stick, 2 inches
	1 lemon

Put the fruits in a medium-size bowl, cover with cold water, and soak for at least 12 hours or overnight. Drain the fruits in a colander and discard the soaking water.

Pour 1¾ cups fresh water into a large saucepan and add the red wine, sugar and cinnamon stick. Use a swivel peeler to remove the lemon rind and cut it into thin strips. Add to the saucepan. Bring to a boil over moderate heat and stir until the sugar is dissolved. Add the drained fruits, reduce heat to low, and simmer for 10 to 15 minutes, until fruits are tender when pierced with a fork. Using a slotted spoon, transfer fruits to a deep serving dish. Cover the dish with foil to keep the fruits warm. Discard the cinnamon stick.

Return saucepan to high heat and boil the syrup for about 30 minutes, until it thickens a little and is somewhat reduced in volume. Strain the syrup over the fruits in the serving dish. If you wish to serve the fruits hot, serve immediately. To serve cold, chill in the refrigerator for at least 1 hour.

Pear Compote

4 portions

4 ripe firm pears
¾ cup sugar
1 teaspoon vanilla extract

rind of 1 lemon
2 tablespoons halved glacé cherries

Wash pears, peel them, removing the thinnest possible layer of peel, quarter them, and cut out cores. Pour 1¼ cups water into a large heavy saucepan; add the sugar and vanilla and bring to a boil over moderate heat. Stir the mixture until the sugar is dissolved. Rub the pears gently but firmly with the lemon rind and add pears and rind to the saucepan. Reduce heat to low and simmer for 10 to 15 minutes, until pears are tender but not mushy. Remove pan from heat and let the pears cool in the syrup for 30 minutes.

Transfer pears with a slotted spoon to a deep serving dish. Discard lemon rind. Arrange the cherry halves in the dish with the pears.

Return saucepan to heat and boil the syrup over high heat until it thickens a little and is reduced in volume. Pour the syrup over the pears in the dish and chill in the refrigerator for at least 1 hour. Serve cold. Also nice with whipped cream.

Variation: Substitute peaches or apples for the pears.

Rhubarb and Orange Compote

6 portions

1 pound rhubarb
1 cup sugar

3 large seedless oranges

Discard rhubarb leaves, trim root ends, and wipe the stalks with a clean damp cloth. Cut the stalks at an angle into 1-inch slices and place them in a heavy saucepan or flameproof casserole. Sprinkle ½ cup of the sugar over the rhubarb and add the grated rind of 1 orange. Cover pan and set aside for 1 hour to draw out the juices.

Place saucepan over low heat or in an oven heated to 350°F. Stew rhubarb gently for 5 to 10 minutes. Shake the pan occasionally if cooking on top of the stove to help fruit cook evenly. Taste and add remaining sugar if necessary. Continue stewing for 5 minutes longer on top of the stove, or

for 10 minutes longer in the oven. Test for tenderness by inserting a sharp knife into a piece of rhubarb; it should offer no resistance. Leave the saucepan uncovered in a cool place until fruit is cold.

Prepare the oranges. Cut a slice from the bottom of each one, then cut away the peel in a spiral, removing all the bitter-tasting white portion and a little of the fruit in the process. Divide the oranges into segments by cutting between the membranes, then around the outer rim. When rhubarb is cold, add orange segments and squeeze the juice from the orange membranes over the dish.

Variation: For richer flavor, pour the juices from the cooked rhubarb into a saucepan. Add the juice of 1 orange and boil rapidly to reduce the juices to a thicker syrup.

Poached Blueberries

6 portions

2 pints blueberries
2 cups sugar

grated rind of 1 lemon
½ teaspoon ground cinnamon

Wash blueberries, discard any stems, leaves or green berries, and drain them well. Combine the sugar with ½ cup water, the lemon rind and cinnamon in a heavy saucepan. Bring to a boil and boil for 1 minute. Add blueberries, reduce heat,

and simmer berries for about 5 minutes. Let the berries cool in the syrup.

Serve with cream, whipped cream, sour cream, yogurt or ice cream.

Golden Oranges

4 portions

6 large oranges	1 tablespoon chopped candied orange peel
4 tablespoons butter	
2 tablespoons honey	½ cup plain yogurt

Cut the rind and white portion of peel from 4 of the oranges. Cut the fruit into ½-inch slices; remove seeds and the white center of each slice. Squeeze the juice from remaining oranges.

Melt 2 tablespoons of the butter in a large frying pan over high heat. Put in as many orange slices as will fit in a single layer. Brown them on both sides, turning carefully.

Remove and keep warm. Add more butter to the pan if necessary and cook remaining orange slices. Return all the oranges to the pan and spoon in the honey. Pour in the orange juice and allow the liquid to bubble for 1 minute. Transfer everything to a warmed serving dish. Scatter the candied peel over the top. Serve the yogurt separately.

Variation: For tipsy golden oranges, omit the orange juice and warm ¼ cup Grand Marnier or brandy while browning the oranges. Ignite the spirit and pour over the orange slices after they have been sweetened. When the flames die down, transfer oranges to a warmed serving dish.

Peaches in Red-Currant Sauce

4 portions

4 large or 8 small peaches	3 tablespoons butter
4 tablespoons red-currant jelly	2 ounces slivered blanched almonds or sunflower seeds
¼ cup dry red wine	

Cover the peaches with boiling water and leave for 3 minutes. Drain and peel the peaches, and leave until completely cold. Halve and pit the peaches and cut them lengthwise into ½-inch slices.

Melt the red-currant jelly with the wine over low heat. Melt 2 tablespoons of the butter in a large frying pan over high heat. Put in half of the peach slices and brown them on both sides. Transfer them to a plate and keep warm. Melt remaining butter if necessary and cook remaining peach slices. Return all the peaches to the frying pan. Pour in the jelly mixture and let the syrup bubble for 30 seconds. Transfer everything to a warmed serving dish. Scatter almonds or sunflower seeds over the top.

Peaches in Brandy

makes about 4 pints

2 pounds small peaches	2 cups brandy
6 cups sugar	

Place the peaches in a large heatproof bowl and pour in enough boiling water to cover them. After 3 minutes, remove the peaches with a slotted spoon to a bowl. Discard blanching water. Peel the peaches, cut them into halves, and remove and discard the pits.

Pour the sugar into a large saucepan and add 5 cups water. Over low heat, stir constantly until sugar is dissolved.

Increase heat to moderate and bring the syrup to a boil. Carefully lower the peach halves into the syrup and poach them for 1 minute. Remove pan from heat. With a slotted spoon lift peaches out of the syrup and place them in sterilized hot preserving jars, filling the jars three-quarters full.

Pour 2½ cups of the syrup into a medium-size saucepan. Discard remaining syrup, or refrigerate and save for other uses. Over moderately high heat bring the syrup to a boil, stirring occasionally. Boil the syrup without stirring until it registers 220°F on a candy thermometer, or until a teaspoon of the syrup dropped into cold water forms a soft ball when rolled between your fingertips.

Remove pan from heat and stir in the brandy. Combine well, and divide the syrup among the preserving jars. Seal the jars with their vacuum lids and store them in a cool dry place for at least 4 months before using.

Pears Poached in Red Wine

6 portions

6	large firm pears	1	cinnamon stick, 2 inches
1	lemon	½	cup red wine
¾	cup sugar		

Use a sharp stainless-steel knife to peel the pears. With a swivel peeler remove the rind of the lemon in 1 long strip. Place pears, lemon rind, the sugar, ½ cup water and the cinnamon stick in a large saucepan. Set the pan over moderate heat, cover, and cook the pears for 10 minutes. Add the wine, reduce heat to very low, and simmer, turning pears occasionally, for 20 to 25 minutes longer, until pears are tender but still firm. Use a slotted spoon to transfer pears to a serving dish.

Increase heat to high and boil the syrup for 8 minutes, until it has thickened slightly. Remove pan from heat and strain the syrup over the pears. Set the dish aside at room temperature until the pears are cool. Chill them in the refrigerator for at least 1 hour before serving.

Peach Melba

6 portions

3	large peaches	½	cup red-currant jelly
¾	cup sugar	1½	teaspoons cornstarch
1	1-inch piece of vanilla bean	1	pint vanilla ice cream
1	package (10 ounces) frozen raspberries		

Blanch and peel the peaches, halve them, and remove pits. Poach the peach halves in a syrup made of the sugar, 1 cup water and the piece of vanilla bean. Let them cool in the syrup, then drain them.

Place raspberries in a saucepan and let them thaw. Mash the berries with a spoon or fork, add the jelly, and bring to a boil over low heat. Mix the cornstarch with 1 tablespoon cold water and stir the mixture into the raspberries. Cook, stirring, until the mixture is clear. Strain the sauce and cool it.

Place a scoop of ice cream in a sundae glass or small glass dish. Top the ice cream with a peach half, pitted side down. Pour sauce over each peach and serve immediately.

Pears Paradiso

4 portions

4	large firm pears	2	tablespoons orange-flavored liqueur (Grand Marnier)
1	tablespoon lemon juice		
2	tablespoons chopped candied lemon peel	2	tablespoons sugar
2	tablespoons chopped walnuts	⅔	cup orange juice

Peel the pears, halve them, and remove cores. Lay the pear halves, cut sides up, in a baking dish. Sprinkle with lemon juice. Combine the candied lemon peel, chopped walnuts and liqueur in a small mixing bowl. Spoon the mixture into the pear hollows. Combine 1 tablespoon of the sugar with the orange juice in a small saucepan over low heat. Stir until the sugar is dissolved. Increase heat to moderate and bring orange juice to a boil. Remove pan from heat and pour the sweetened juice around the pears. Cover the baking dish and place in the oven. Bake the pears for 1 hour at 350°F, basting occasionally.

Preheat broiler to high. Remove baking dish from the oven, remove cover, and sprinkle remaining sugar on top of the pears. Slide the dish under the broiler and broil for 2 to 3 minutes, until pears are golden brown. Remove pears from the broiler and serve immediately.

Caramel Pears

6 portions

12	small pears	1¾	cups dry white wine
¾	cup sugar	12	ladyfingers

Wash pears, peel them carefully without removing the stems, and core them from the base, removing the smallest possible amount of pear around the core. Combine sugar and wine in a large saucepan and dissolve the sugar over low heat, stirring constantly. When sugar is dissolved, place the pears in the pan. Poach the pears, basting them frequently, for 15 to 20 minutes, until they are tender but still hold their shape.

Arrange the ladyfingers, split open, on a serving dish.

Remove pears from the syrup and arrange them on top of the ladyfingers.

Increase heat to moderate and boil the syrup for 8 to 10 minutes, until it turns a light golden brown. Do not let it darken too much, or it will become too stiff. Remove pan from heat. Spoon enough of the syrup over the pears to glaze them. Let them cool completely before serving, 2 pears for each portion. Accompany with heavy cream, plain or lightly whipped.

Pears Baked with Cardamom

6 portions

3   large pears
2   tablespoons soft brown
     sugar
½   cup orange-flavored liqueur
     (Grand Marnier)

2   teaspoons ground
     cardamom
1¼ cups heavy cream

Preheat oven to 350°F. Peel the pears, halve them, and remove cores. Use a sharp stainless-steel knife to slice the pears. Arrange slices in a shallow ovenproof dish and sprinkle them with the sugar. Pour the liqueur over the top, then sprinkle with the cardamom. Place the dish in the oven and bake for 35 to 40 minutes, until pear slices are tender.

Remove dish from oven and transfer fruit to individual dessert dishes. Set aside to cool completely. When pears are cold, spoon equal amounts of the cream, plain or lightly whipped, into each dish and serve at once.

Poires Belle-Hélène

4 to 8 portions

4 large ripe pears	1½ cups chocolate sauce
¾ cup sugar	1½ pints vanilla ice cream
1 vanilla bean, split	

Peel the pears with a stainless-steel knife, halve them, and remove cores. Combine sugar, 1½ cups water and the split vanilla bean in a large heavy saucepan. Dissolve the sugar over low heat, stirring constantly. When sugar is dissolved, increase heat to moderate and boil the syrup for 2 minutes, without stirring. Remove the vanilla bean, rinse it in hot water, and save to use again. Reduce heat to low, add the pear halves, and poach them for 12 to 15 minutes, until they are tender but still firm. Remove pan from heat and set pears aside to cool in the syrup.

Transfer pears and syrup to a large bowl and place in the refrigerator. Chill pears for 30 minutes.

Just before serving, heat the chocolate sauce. Scoop vanilla ice cream into a chilled serving dish. Remove the bowl of pears from the refrigerator. Use a slotted spoon to lift pear halves from the syrup and arrange them around the ice cream. (Strain the syrup, chill, and reserve for another use.) Pour the hot chocolate sauce into a warmed sauceboat, or over the pears, and serve immediately.

Raspberry Fool

4 portions

2 pints fresh raspberries	1½ cups heavy cream
1 cup sugar	1 tablespoon brandy

Wash the raspberries in a strainer and let them drain well. Place them in a mixing bowl and sprinkle with the sugar. Set aside for 2 hours.

Mash the raspberries with a kitchen fork until they are reduced to a pulp. Whip the cream until soft peaks form, then fold cream and brandy into the raspberries and mix until well blended. Spoon the mixture into a glass serving bowl and place in the refrigerator to chill for 1 hour.

Remove the bowl from the refrigerator and serve immediately.

Raspberries with Ice Cream and Maraschino

4 portions

½ cup sugar
2 teaspoons grated lemon
   rind
3 tablespoons maraschino
   liqueur

2 pints fresh raspberries
2 tablespoons sliced
   almonds
1 pint vanilla ice cream

Place 4 sundae glasses in the refrigerator to chill. Make the syrup: Combine the sugar, ½ cup water and the grated lemon rind in a saucepan over low heat and cook, stirring constantly, until sugar is dissolved. Increase heat to moderately high and boil the syrup, without stirring, for 4 minutes. Remove pan from heat and set the syrup aside to cool completely.

Strain the syrup into a mixing bowl and stir in the maraschino, raspberries and sliced almonds. Chill the mixture in the refrigerator for 30 minutes, stirring occasionally.

Remove sundae glasses and the bowl of raspberries from the refrigerator. Divide raspberries evenly among the 4 glasses. Using an ice-cream scoop, place a ball of ice cream in each glass. Serve immediately.

Strawberries Romanoff

4 to 6 portions

2	quarts fresh strawberries
½	cup orange-flavored liqueur
¼	cup strained orange juice

1¼	cups heavy cream
2	tablespoons superfine sugar
1	teaspoon vanilla extract

Wash and hull the strawberries. Let them drain well, or roll in paper towels to dry. Place strawberries in a deep bowl and pour the orange-flavored liqueur and orange juice over them. Cover the bowl and place in the refrigerator. Chill the strawberries for 2 hours, basting them occasionally with the liquid in the bowl. Transfer strawberries and liquid to a serving dish.

Whip the cream until it thickens, then add the sugar, ½ tablespoon at a time, and the vanilla, and beat until the sugar is dissolved and the cream is in soft peaks; this is *crème Chantilly*. Fill a pastry bag with the *crème Chantilly* and pipe it around the berries, or in decorative swirls over the top of them. Serve at once.

Pineapple Flamed with Kirsch

4 portions

1	medium to large pineapple
3	tablespoons butter
¼	cup kirsch
¼	cup sugar

1	tablespoon chopped candied angelica or other candied fruit

Peel the pineapple. Cut the fruit into ½-inch slices and cut out the cores. Melt half of the butter in a large frying pan over high heat. Put in as many pineapple slices as will fit in a single layer. Brown them on both sides. Remove slices and keep warm. Add more butter to the pan if necessary and brown the rest of the slices.

Pour the liqueur into a small pan and warm it over low heat. Return all pineapple slices to the frying pan and sprinkle in the sugar. Ignite the kirsch and pour it over the pineapple. As soon as the flames die, transfer everything to a warmed serving dish. Scatter the angelica over the top. Serve at once.

Part Five
A GREEK FEAST

The music, and the banquet, and the wine—
The garlands, the rose odours, and the flowers—
The sparkling eyes, and flashing ornaments—
Byron

There are as many reasons and occasions for a feast as there are days in the year. Aside from national and religious holidays, there are more intimate family events that call for recognition and celebration—a birthday, graduation, anniversary, a goal achieved, an honor or a prize bestowed. Perhaps the best reason of all to plan a feast is to rejoice in the reunion of family and friends, to welcome home, to revel and enjoy the pleasure of each other's company.

Our menu for a Greek feast captures the sun-filled flavors, the heady and robust aromas of the fabled Greek Isles. The scent of rosemary, orégano and mint mingle with lemon, cinnamon and pungent garlic. Most of the ingredients for this flavorful feast can be purchased in a good supermarket. Look for the phyllo dough in the refrigerator compartment or in the frozen food section. Grape leaves preserved in brine are sold in 1-pound jars in the section that carries other imported delicacies, and almost every delicatessen section carries feta cheese.

The Greek word *mezethakia* means "something to whet the appetite," and this you will unfailingly achieve with the two appetizers that start the meal and set the stage for the remainder of the feast. The *tiropetes* are tiny triangles of feta cheese wrapped in layers of delicate and flaky phyllo pastry. The *dolmades* are grape leaves stuffed with a mixture of rice, currants, herbs and spices, then slowly simmered in lemon juice and olive oil. They are intended to be eaten cold; the combined flavors of subtle sweetness and pungent tartness are delicious. The *tiropetes* may be made ahead and frozen, to be baked quickly minutes before serving. *Dolmades* must be made ahead, at least one day and better three, to reach their full blend of flavors.

A roasted joint of meat has been the traditional centerpiece of almost any Western feast, and in our menu the leg of lamb superbly fills this role. The meat is flavored with garlic and herbs and enhanced by a final addition of onions and potatoes, roasted with the meat during the final half hour. Ripe red tomatoes are topped with fragrant olive oil and rosemary and briefly broiled.

No Greek meal is complete without a crisp salad made of lettuces and other raw vegetables. Ignore, for once, the rules that say to tear your lettuce into bite-size pieces; instead do as they do in Greece—chop the lettuce into ribbons with a sharp kitchen knife. You'll be amazed to discover that shredded lettuce has a texture unlike that prepared any other way. Fresh herbs—mint and parsley—are added to enhance the flavor of the salad.

Our feast comes to a splendid end with a refreshing macédoine of fruits accompanied by crescent-shaped butter cookies called *koura-biedes*.

To serve a feast implies more than the cooking of a lavish meal; it is not unlike the staging of a play. It is your own production and requires careful planning. The host or hostess must be the producer, director, set designer and actor in the leading role.

Put out your gayest table linens, serve wine in brightly colored jugs, gather fresh herbs and simple flowers to decorate the table. Light many candles, dim the lights, play hot bouzouki music on the stereo, and then relax with family and friends. Eat, drink, talk, dance—enjoy the feast!

A GREEK FEAST FOR 10 TO 12

Tiropetes
Dolmades
Roast Leg of Lamb
With Onions and Potatoes
Broiled Tomatoes Scented with Rosemary
Greek Salad
Macédoine of Fruits
Kourabiedes

***

Wine Suggestion
Apéritif: Ouzo
Wine: Retsina or Roditys, Chilled
Liqueur: Metaxa Brandy

Greek Wines and Spirits

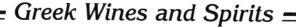

Although wine was probably introduced into France by the Greeks when they colonized the area around present-day Marseilles in 600 B.C., we are today less familiar with the products of Grecian vineyards than we are with those of almost any other country. Ancient Greek wines were very sweet, strong in alcohol, and highly flavored with herbs and flowers. Today the Greeks still like to flavor much of their wine with resin, a flavor that comes as something of a shock to those who have never tasted it. Retsina, the name of any wine flavored with resin, is an acquired taste.

Greek rosé, such as roditys, is light, dry and extremely pleasing as an all-purpose wine. Some of the finer brands to look for are Achaia-Clauss, Marko, Cambas and Evi-Evan. These wines are best served slightly chilled; they can be served with almost any type of food.

The most popular drink in every sidewalk café, on every sun-drenched island throughout Greece, is a small glass of licorice-flavored ouzo. Distilled from grape mash, ouzo is similar in flavor to Pernod, Ricard and pastis. Ouzo is extremely potent despite its innocent taste. Its alcoholic content runs to 100 proof. It is the traditional drink to sip with Greek appetizers. Serve it with or without ice, but always with a small pitcher of water. Each person dilutes his own glass of ouzo with water, which turns the clear liquid to a cloudy, milky white.

Metaxa brandy is the traditional after-dinner liqueur. The color is a dark amber and the taste is somewhat sweet.

MARKET LIST

Meat

1   leg of lamb, 7 to 8 pounds

Fruits and Vegetables

1   bunch of fresh mint
3   tablespoons dried mint
2   bunches of fresh parsley
3   bunches of scallions
5   lemons
9   ripe tomatoes
1   head of garlic
5   large onions

20   small potatoes
1   bunch of fresh rosemary or dried rosemary
1   head of romaine lettuce
1   head of escarole lettuce
1   medium-size cucumber
1   large green pepper
1   bunch of radishes

1   red onion
4   ounces black Kalamata olives
1   pint strawberries
1   pound seedless green grapes
3   ripe peaches
2   bananas

Staples

olive oil
unsalted butter
long-grain rice
dried currants
eggs
ground cinnamon
ground allspice
granulated sugar
superfine sugar
confectioners' sugar

coarse (kosher) salt
orégano
black peppercorns
dry vermouth
Grand Marnier liqueur
brandy
vanilla extract
cake flour
cream cheese

Specialty Items

½   pound phyllo dough, also called *filo* (12 sheets)
1   pound grapevine leaves, preserved in brine
¾   pound feta cheese

Tiropetes

These are tiny pastry triangles made of phyllo dough and filled with feta cheese. They may be prepared ahead and frozen, unbaked, until you need them. Brush them with *melted butter and bake them, unthawed, in a 375°F oven for about 20 minutes, until they are puffed and golden brown.*

36 pastry triangles

8 ounces feta cheese
3 ounces cream cheese
1 large egg
¼ cup minced fresh mint or parsley
    freshly ground black pepper
½ pound phyllo dough (12 sheets), thawed if it has been frozen
4 ounces unsalted butter, melted

Combine the feta cheese, cream cheese, egg and mint or parsley in the bowl of an electric mixer or food processor and blend until creamy. Season with freshly ground pepper to taste.

Bring the phyllo to room temperature, and work with 1 sheet at a time; keep the others covered with a slightly damp towel to prevent drying. Brush each sheet of pastry lightly with melted butter and cut the sheet into 3 long strips, each about 4 inches wide. Fold each strip lengthwise in half, buttered side in. Brush the top side with melted butter. Place 1 tablespoon of the cheese mixture on the bottom corner of a buttered strip and fold the strip over to make a right-angled triangle. Continue folding the strip, making right-angled turns, as if folding a flag, to the end, so the triangle is made of many pastry layers. Brush with melted butter. Continue until all sheets are buttered and cut into strips, then folded, buttered, filled and made into triangles. Place the pastries on a lightly buttered or nonstick baking sheet and bake in a preheated 375°F oven for 15 to 20 minutes, until pastries have puffed and turned golden brown. Serve warm.

Dolmades

Grape leaves stuffed with rice and spices, dolmades are served cold or at room temperature. Make them at least a *day ahead, or as long as 3 or 4 days before they are to be served.*

40 to 50 stuffed grape leaves

1 jar (1 pound) grape leaves, preserved in brine
1 cup long-grain rice
2 to 3 bunches of scallions
3 ripe tomatoes
3 tablespoons crushed dried mint
3 tablespoons minced fresh parsley
½ cup dried currants
½ teaspoon ground cinnamon
½ teaspoon ground allspice
    freshly ground black pepper
    juice of 2 large lemons
½ cup olive oil
1 tablespoon sugar
12 garlic cloves, unpeeled
1 lemon, sliced into thin rounds

Remove grape leaves from the jar, separate them carefully, and rinse them under running water to remove excess salt. Bring 3 quarts water to a boil and put the rice in the boiling water. Turn off the heat, stir rice, and let it soak for 5 minutes. Drain, rinse with cold water, and drain again. Chop enough of the scallions, including green parts, to make 1 cup. Blanch and peel the tomatoes and chop fine. Mix drained rice, chopped scallions and tomatoes, mint, parsley, currants, cinnamon, allspice and pepper to taste in a large bowl.

Place the grape leaves on a board, with the top side down. Place 1 heaping teaspoon of the rice mixture on the leaf, near the stem. Fold leaf over, fold in the sides, and roll up the leaf tightly to enclose the filling completely. Continue until all the filling or the unbroken grape leaves are used. Arrange dolmades seam sides down to fit snugly in a baking dish. Combine lemon juice, olive oil and sugar and pour over the dolmades. Tuck the garlic cloves in among the grape leaves. Cover tightly with foil, and bake in a 325°F oven for 2 hours. Check frequently and add water if liquid is evaporating.

Cool the grape leaves completely before refrigerating them. Serve cold, garnished with lemon slices.

Roast Leg of Lamb with Onions and Potatoes

10 to 12 portions

1 leg of lamb, 7 to 8 pounds
3 garlic cloves
juice of 1 lemon
1 tablespoon dried orégano
1 tablespoon coarse salt

1 tablespoon freshly ground
black pepper
½ cup dry vermouth
20 small potatoes
4 or 5 large onions

Trim the lamb of all visible fat. Peel garlic cloves and cut into thin slivers. Insert garlic slivers into the meat all over, making incisions with a sharp knife. Rub entire surface with lemon juice, then rub in the orégano, salt and pepper. Insert a meat thermometer, not touching bone or fat. Place the lamb in a roasting pan and roast in a preheated 325°F oven for about 2 hours. Subtract 15 minutes if you like it rare and add 15 minutes if you like it well done. (The internal temperature should be 145°F for medium-rare, 160°F for medium, or 170°F for well done.) Baste the lamb every 30 minutes with a little vermouth.

Peel potatoes and onions and cut into 1-inch-thick slices. Arrange vegetables in the roasting pan around the lamb about 30 minutes before it should be done. Baste the vegetables with drippings from the lamb. When lamb is done, remove it to a platter and let it rest for 15 to 20 minutes.

While lamb rests, continue cooking the vegetables. Arrange the roast on a large platter, surrounded by the oven-roasted vegetables.

Broiled Tomatoes Scented with Rosemary

10 to 12 portions

6 large ripe tomatoes
olive oil

several sprigs of fresh
rosemary, or 1
tablespoon dried

Cut tomatoes across into halves and arrange them on an oiled baking pan. Stick 6 or 7 rosemary leaves into each tomato half, or sprinkle with dried, and drizzle with a little olive oil. Place under the broiler and broil for 4 to 5 minutes, until tomatoes are heated through. Serve tomatoes with the roast lamb.

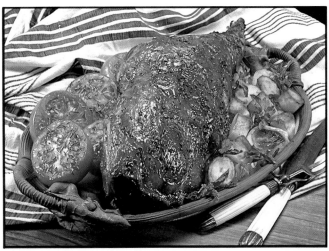

Greek Salad

10 to 12 portions

1	large head of romaine	1	bunch of parsley
1	head of escarole	1	large handful of fresh mint
1	cucumber		leaves, or 1 tablespoon
1	large green pepper		crushed dried mint
1	bunch of radishes	4	ounces black Kalamata olives
1	red onion	4	ounces feta cheese

Separate leaves of romaine and escarole; wash well and dry them. Cut leaves into ½-inch-wide ribbons and place in a large salad bowl. Peel cucumber. Wash and halve green pepper, and discard stem, seeds and ribs. Wash and stem radishes. Peel the red onion. Cut all these vegetables into thin slices. Wash and dry parsley and mint, discard all stems, and chop leaves fine. Halve and pit the olives. Crumble the feta cheese. Add all these ingredients to the lettuces and chill the salad in the refrigerator until ready to serve.

Lemon and Oil Dressing

¾	cup olive oil	salt and pepper
¼	cup lemon juice	

Mix oil and lemon juice together and add salt and freshly ground pepper to taste. Pour on the salad just before serving.

Toss well to coat all ingredients and serve.

Kourabiedes

These Greek butter cookies can be made 1 week ahead.

4 dozen cookies

1	pound unsalted butter, at room temperature	1½	tablespoons vanilla extract
¾	cup confectioners' sugar	4½	cups sifted cake flour
1	egg yolk		additional confectioners' sugar for topping

Place butter and ¾ cup sugar in the bowl of an electric mixer and cream until very light. Add egg yolk and vanilla and cream until well blended. Continue beating as you gradually add the flour, until it is all incorporated; the dough should be soft without being sticky.

Preheat oven to 350°F. Dip hands into flour and shape the dough into balls the size of a walnut, then shape each ball into a small crescent. Place on ungreased baking sheets and bake for 15 minutes, until cookies turn a light sandy color. Let them cool. Sift additional confectioners' sugar generously over the tops.

Macédoine of Fruits

The combination of fruits is merely one suggestion out of many possible choices. Make substitutions based on flavor, availability and freshness. This can be served chilled or flambéed.

10 to 12 portions

1 pint strawberries
1 pound seedless green
   grapes
2 or 3 ripe peaches
2 ripe bananas

1 cup superfine sugar
¼ cup Grand Marnier liqueur
   or brandy
¼ cup brandy for flaming
   (optional)

Wash and hull strawberries. Wash grapes and remove from stems. Peel and slice peaches and bananas. Mix the fruits together in a glass or crystal bowl. Sprinkle with sugar and drizzle with ¼ cup liqueur or brandy. Cover and chill for 2 to 3 hours before serving.

For added drama, serve the macédoine of fruits aflame with spirits. Arrange the fruits in a flameproof bowl. Bring back to room temperature after chilling. Warm an additional ¼ cup brandy in a small saucepan over low heat for 1 minute. Pour brandy over the fruit and ignite with a match. Take care to stand well back as mixture will burst into flames. Serve as soon as the flames have died down.

INDEX